Butterworths Tax Studies

Purchase by a Company of its Own Shares

A Guide to Company Law and Tax Law

Deloitte Haskins + Sells
Chartered Accountants

London
Butterworths
1983

England	Butterworth & Co (Publishers) Ltd 88 Kingsway, London WC2B 6AB
Australia	Butterworths Pty Ltd 271–273 Lane Cove Road, North Ryde Sydney, NSW 2113 Also at Melbourne, Brisbane, Adelaide and Perth
Canada	Butterworth & Co (Canada) Ltd 2265 Midland Avenue, Scarborough Ontario, M1P 4S1
	Butterworth & Co (Western Canada) 409 Granville Street, Ste 856 Vancouver BC, V6C 1T2
New Zealand	Butterworths of New Zealand Ltd 33–35 Cumberland Place, Wellington
Singapore	Butterworth & Co (Asia) Pte Ltd Crawford Post Office Box 770, Singapore 9119
South Africa	Butterworth & Co (South Africa) (Pty) Ltd Box No 792, Durban
USA	Mason Publishing Co Finch Building, 366 Wacouta Street St Paul, Minnesota 55101
	Butterworth (Legal Publishers) Inc 15014 NE 40th, Suite 205, Redmond, Washington 98052
	Butterworth (Legal Publishers) Inc 381 Elliot Street, Newton, Upper Falls Massachusetts 02164

© Deloitte Haskins + Sells 1983

ISBN 0 406 25268 8

Printed & bound in Great Britain by Billing & Sons Ltd., Worcester

Foreword

Butterworths Tax Studies is a new series of concise texts on subjects of topical interest. The titles selected will generally cover very specific areas of practice or concern, drawing together material from a variety of sources, so that transactions can be evaluated in terms of their overall tax implications. Where appropriate, related legal and accounting aspects will also be considered.

Butterworth & Co (Publishers) Ltd

Preface

The general rule that prevented a company buying its own shares was established in 1887 by the case of Trevor v Whitworth. In the United States and in Europe, however, a company is, subject to certain restrictions, generally permitted to purchase its own shares. The Jenkins Committee in 1962 examined the case for change and found there was nothing inherently wrong in permitting companies to purchase their own shares. But, because there was no evidence that British companies needed the power, they recommended that the general prohibition should be retained. In recent years, there has been a growing number of representations to the effect that the facility for a company to purchase its own shares should be available to companies in the UK. The main issues involved were discussed in the Consultative Document 'The purchase by a company of its own shares' (Cmnd. 7944) that was published in June 1980. The Companies Act 1981 gives companies the power to purchase their own shares, subject to certain restrictions.

In September 1981, the Inland Revenue issued a Consultative Document entitled 'Companies purchasing their own shares: implications for corporation tax, income tax and capital gains tax'. As a result, the Finance Act 1982 contains amendments to the tax law.

A company's power to purchase its own shares should have advantages, in particular, for private companies. It has often been difficult to transfer shares in private companies. This has resulted in shareholders becoming 'locked in' (that is, unable to sell their shares and recover their investment). Now, a company may use its power to purchase its own shares to enable a shareholder to realise his investment. In addition, a family company can exercise this new power to retain family control by using company funds to purchase the shares of either a retiring or a deceased family member.

The advantages are, perhaps, less significant for public companies than for private companies, but they are nonetheless real. In particular, public companies will be able to return surplus funds to shareholders by purchasing and cancelling some of their shares. Also, the new power will provide public companies with flexibility both in ordering their capital structure and in matching that structure to their needs at any stage of their development.

This booklet is a practical guide to both the company law and the tax law that apply when any company purchases its own shares. It also covers various connected matters, for example, contingent purchase contracts, the requirements of The Stock Exchange, acquisitions other than purchases, and practical points on the implementation of the tax law provisions. It is divided into six parts as follows:

(a)   Part I illustrates the application of the provisions of company law and tax law by means of a private, unquoted company's purchase of its own shares.

(b)   Part II contains a detailed explanation of all the provisions of company law and tax law that apply when a private, unquoted company purchases its own shares.

(c)   Part III explains the different provisions of company law and tax law that apply when either a public, unquoted company or a public, quoted company purchases its own shares.

(d)   Part IV explains contingent purchase contracts, the assignment or the release of a company's right to purchase its own shares, payments for transactions other than purchases, the requirements of the City Code on Take-overs and Mergers and the requirements of The Stock Exchange.

(e)   Part V comments on acquisitions other than purchases and, in particular, on redeemable shares.

(f)   Part VI discusses several important practical points that may emerge from the implementation of the tax law provisions.

(g)   Appendix I comprises a checklist of the requirements of the Companies Act 1981 that apply when either a private company or a public company purchases its own shares.

(h)   Appendix II illustrates the prescribed form for a return by a company purchasing its own shares.

(i)   Appendix III comprises a checklist of the requirements of the Companies Act 1981 that apply when a private company purchases its own shares out of capital.

(j)   Appendix IV illustrates the prescribed form for the declaration a private company must make in relation to the purchase or the redemption of its shares out of capital.

(k)   Appendix V illustrates the prescribed form for the notice of application a private company must make to the court to cancel a resolution for the purchase or the redemption of its shares out of capital.

(l)   Appendix VI comprises guidance to assist a company when it prepares an application to the Inland Revenue for advance clearance under Finance Act 1982, Schedule 9, Paragraphs 10(1) and 10(2).

Deloitte Haskins + Sells

Contents

Part VI

Part I

This part contains an illustration of the application of the provisions of company law and tax law by means of a private, unquoted company's purchase of its own shares.

Introduction

1.01 The Companies Act 1981 gives any company that has a share capital the power to purchase its own shares subject to certain restrictions. The purpose of the restrictions is to protect both the creditors of the company and those members of the company whose shares are not being purchased. The provisions apply to purchases made on or after 15 June 1982.

1.02 Provisions in the Finance Act 1982 reduce the amount of tax payable when an unquoted company purchases its own shares in certain circumstances. (For this purpose, a company is unquoted either if it has no class of shares listed in the official list of a stock exchange or if it is the subsidiary of such a company.) The provisions apply to purchases made on or after 6 April 1982.

1.03 The provisions of company law and tax law are discussed in detail in Parts II and III of the booklet.

1.04 The remainder of this part of the booklet illustrates the way in which the provisions apply when a private, unquoted company makes an uncomplicated purchase of its own shares.

Application of the company law provisions

1.05 Z Limited (Z) (a private, unquoted company) is a long-established family manufacturing company. Mr. Brown (a director of Z) purchased for £10,000 many years ago 10,000 of Z's 100,000 issued ordinary £1 shares. He has now had a major disagreement with his fellow directors about the way in which Z is run. The directors and the other shareholders have agreed that it is in everyone's best interests for Mr. Brown to sever his links with the company. He will resign as a director, and the company will purchase his shares from him for £24,000 (which is the agreed market value). The company will make the payment out of distributable profits.

1.06 At present, Z's articles of association do not permit it to purchase its own shares. This means that Z cannot proceed with the purchase until it alters its articles of association. This will require a special resolution.

1

1.07   Z can purchase Mr. Brown's shares only under a contract. The terms of this contract will need to be authorised by a special resolution of the company. (Mr. Brown cannot vote on this special resolution.)

1.08   The terms of the contract will need to include, *inter alia*, a description of, and the number of, the shares to be purchased, the amount of the payment, the date of the purchase and a statement that payment will be made at the time of the purchase. (The company can then purchase Mr. Brown's shares at any time after the date of the special resolution to authorise the contract.)

1.09   If the special resolution is to be effective, Z will need to make the contract available for inspection both at its registered office during the 15 days immediately preceding the meeting that will consider the special resolution, and at the meeting itself.

1.10   Within 28 days of the date on which Mr. Brown's shares are delivered to Z, the company will need to make a return to the Registrar of Companies. This return must be in the prescribed form, and it must state the following:

(a)   The number and the nominal value of the shares purchased.

(b)   The date on which the shares were delivered to the company.

1.11   In addition, Z will need to keep the contract for the purchase at its registered office for 10 years from the date of the purchase. Throughout this time, the contract must be available during business hours for members to inspect.

1.12   In their report attached to the financial statements that relate to the year when the purchase took place, the directors will have to state the following details in respect of the purchase:

(a)   The number and the nominal value of the shares the company purchased, and the percentage of the called-up capital of that description that these shares represent.

(b)   The aggregate consideration the company paid and the reasons for the purchase.

1.13   Z must treat Mr. Brown's shares as being cancelled on purchase. Because the company made the payment out of distributable profits, Z will need to transfer £10,000 (that is, the nominal value of the shares purchased) to the capital redemption reserve.

1.14   The effect on the balance sheet of Z would be as follows:

Before the purchase, the summarised balance sheet was as shown below:

	£
Share capital	
100,000 ordinary shares of £1 each	100,000
Distributable reserves	50,000
	£150,000

	£
Net assets other than cash	125,000
Cash	25,000
	£150,000

Then, after the purchase, the summarised balance sheet will be:

	£
Share capital	
90,000 ordinary shares of £1 each	90,000
Capital redemption reserve	10,000
Distributable reserves	26,000
	£126,000
Net assets other than cash	125,000
Cash	1,000
	£126,000

Application of the tax law provisions

1.15 The changes in the tax rules are radical. The changes can be explained by considering the effects of both the old tax rules and the new tax rules in the circumstances of the example.

The old tax rules.

1.16 Z paid £24,000 for shares that had originally cost Mr. Brown £10,000. Under the old rules, the gain of £14,000 would be taxed, broadly speaking, as a dividend. This would have important consequences for both Z and Mr. Brown.

1.17 As with any other dividend, Z would be required to pay over to the Inland Revenue advance corporation tax (ACT). In this example, that would mean that Z would pay ACT of £6,000 (that is, 3/7ths of £14,000). Of course, the company could set that ACT against the eventual corporation tax liability on its profits. However, it would at least involve a cash flow disadvantage, because the ACT would be paid many months before the corporation tax liability becomes payable. Furthermore, because of, for example, capital allowances or stock relief, Z might not have an immediate corporation tax liability. This factor would aggravate the cash flow disadvantage. (If Z had a subsidiary, it could surrender the ACT to that subsidiary.)

1.18 Nor would Mr. Brown find his tax position attractive. He would be treated as receiving a cash dividend of £14,000. The tax credit of £6,000 would be added, and this would make a gross taxable dividend of £20,000. This dividend would be fully taxable as income at rates up to 75%, although Mr. Brown would be able to set against that tax a tax credit of 30% of the amount treated as income.

The new tax rules.

1.19 Provided that the requirements in the Finance Act 1982 are satisfied, the payment by Z would not be treated as a dividend. This would have the following consequences.

1.20 Z is not regarded as paying a dividend, and so it would not be required to account for ACT. Similarly, Mr Brown would not be treated as receiving a dividend. However, his shareholding is an asset for capital gains tax purposes, and the gain of £14,000 would be liable to capital gains tax. Even so, he is normally better off because capital gains tax is charged at a maximum of only 30%, whereas the rate of income tax may be higher. The maximum improvement in Mr. Brown's after-tax position (ignoring all exemptions and allowances) would be as shown below:

	£	£
New rules		
Capital gain	14,000	
Capital gains tax @ 30%	4,200	9,800
Old rules		
Dividend	20,000	
Income tax @ 75%	15,000	5,000
Maximum improvement in after-tax position		£4,800

1.21 Thus, the new tax rules result in a substantial improvement in the position of Z and, probably, also of Mr. Brown.

Conclusion

1.22 The example above, which results in a company purchasing its own shares, is a typical situation in which the new provisions might apply. Other circumstances in which the new provisions might apply are considered in the following paragraphs.

1.23 Many companies, particularly family companies, find it difficult to grow beyond a particular level because they need to attract outside finance. Outside investors are often discouraged by the prospect of being 'locked-in' to the company because there is no ready market for their shares. The new provisions are intended to encourage outside investors, because the company itself will be able to provide the market for its shares.

1.24 Another situation in which the new provisions might apply is where either an employee shareholder or a director shareholder retires, and wishes to withdraw from the company completely.

1.25 Finally, family companies often experience difficulties when a major shareholder dies. When this occurs, the surviving members of the family can find that the capital transfer tax liability is such that their only course is to sell the shares to an outsider. This might mean that the family would lose control of the company. Under the new provisions, the company will itself be able to buy those shares, so that the family can retain control of the company. In fact, not only do the new tax rules apply in this case, but the requirements are less stringent. Consequently, this may, in practice, become one of the most important applications of the new provisions.

Part II: Private companies

This part contains a detailed explanation of all the provisions of company law and tax law that apply when a private, unquoted company purchases its own shares.

THE COMPANY LAW PROVISIONS

2.01 Subject to certain conditions, any private company that has a share capital may purchase any of its own shares. This applies whether or not the shares in question are redeemable. If it satisfies the conditions, a private company may purchase its own shares in accordance with the procedures described in this part of the booklet.

The conditions that must be satisfied

2.02 The conditions that a private company must satisfy before it can purchase its own shares are set out in paragraphs 2.03 to 2.13. Appendix I contains a checklist that is designed to assist a company to ensure that it has satisfied all of the relevant conditions. However, in view of the complexity of the legislation, reference should be made to the Companies Act 1981 itself. In addition, professional advice should be sought from solicitors and accountants.

2.03 The company's articles of association must authorise it to purchase its own shares.

2.04 The company must, after the purchase, have other shares in issue, and at least some of these must be not redeemable. Without this condition, the company could redeem its whole share capital and so cease to have any members. This action would negate the effect of provisions in the Companies Act 1948, which provide for sanctions when a company continues to trade with fewer than two members.

2.05 The company must, after the purchase, have at least two members.

2.06 A company may not purchase any of its own shares that are not fully paid.

2.07 The terms of purchase must provide for the shares to be paid for at the time they are purchased. If this restriction did not exist, the company would be able to purchase shares, defer payment and set up a creditor. The company would then still have the benefit of the resources, but without any 'cost'. This would be because creditors do not normally receive interest, whereas dividends are normally paid on shares.

2.08   A private company may purchase its own shares either out of distributable profits or out of the proceeds of a new issue of shares made for the purposes of the purchase. Alternatively, if it is authorised to do so by its articles of association, it may purchase its own shares out of capital (as discussed in paragraphs 2.24 to 2.48).

2.09   Unless the shares that are being purchased were issued at a premium, the company must pay the premium, if any, on purchase out of distributable profits. (For this purpose, the term 'distributable profits' means any profits out of which a company can lawfully make a distribution that is equal in value to the premium on purchase.) Where the shares that the company is purchasing were issued at a premium, the company may pay a proportion of any premium payable on the purchase out of the proceeds of an issue of shares it makes for the purposes of the purchase. This proportion is an amount that does not exceed the lower of the following two amounts:

(a)   The aggregate of the premiums that the company received when it issued the shares that it is now purchasing.

(b)   The amount of the company's share premium account after crediting the premium, if any, on the new issue of shares it makes for the purposes of the purchase.

Where a company pays a part of the premium on purchase out of the proceeds of a new issue, it must reduce its share premium account by an equivalent amount.

If, in the example in Part I of the booklet, Z had purchased Mr. Brown's shares partly out of the proceeds of a new issue of shares and partly out of distributable profits, this calculation can be illustrated as follows:

In January 1950, Z issued 100,000 ordinary shares of £1 each at a premium of 10p per share. After the issue, the balance on Z's share premium account was £10,000.

In January 1952, Z utilised the balance of £10,000 on its share premium account to provide for the premium payable on the redemption of its redeemable preference shares. (No other transaction related to the share premium account during the relevant period.)

In July 1982, Z made an issue of 7,500 ordinary shares of £1 each at a premium of £1 per share for the purposes of purchasing, at a premium of £1.40 per share, Mr. Brown's 10,000 ordinary shares issued in January 1950.

Z may make the purchase in the way shown below:

		£
Out of the issue of shares for the purposes of the purchase:		
Nominal amount of shares purchased		10,000
Premium on purchase. The lower of:		
(a) The premium received on the issue of the shares being purchased (10,000 at 10p)	£1,000	
(b) The balance on the share premium account after the issue of shares for the purchase (see below)	£7,500	

	£
	1,000
	11,000
Out of distributable profits (being the balance of the amount payable on purchase):	13,000
Total payment on purchase (nominal value and premium)	£24,000

The resulting position of the share premium account is as follows:

	£
Share premium account:	
January 1950	10,000
January 1952	(10,000)
	—
July 1982	7,500
Balance after issue of shares for the purchase	7,500
Premium on purchase paid out of proceeds of new issue	(1,000)
Balance carried forward	£6,500

2.10   The company must follow the detailed procedure that the Companies Act 1981 specifies (as discussed in paragraphs 2.17 to 2.20).

2.11   The company must treat the shares it purchases as being cancelled on purchase. Thus, the purchase of shares will reduce the issued share capital by the nominal amount of the shares purchased. However, the purchase will not reduce the authorised share capital. Thus, a company cannot purchase its own shares and hold them as 'treasury shares' until they are resold. By contrast, this practice is permitted, subject to certain limitations, in the USA, and also by the EC Second Directive on the maintenance of share capital. The principal reasons why this practice was rejected in the UK are an aversion to permitting a company to traffic in its shares and (if it were permitted) the complicated problems that would ensue in respect of the accounting treatment of such dealings and the tax treatment of the profits and losses the company made on such dealings.

2.12   In certain circumstances, a company must make a transfer to the capital redemption reserve (as discussed in paragraphs 2.50 to 2.53).

2.13   It should be noted that, where the capital of the company includes shares that have priority on a return of capital over the shares the company proposes to purchase, the company may need to obtain from those shareholders who are entitled to the shares that have priority their consent to a variation of their rights.

The issue of shares for the purposes of a purchase

2.14   Where a company issues shares to raise the proceeds to make a purchase, it can issue shares up to the nominal amount of the shares it is to purchase as if those shares had never been issued. This means that if the nominal value of the company's issued capital is already equal to the nominal value of its authorised capital, a company may (without increasing its authorised capital) still issue new shares for the purposes of the purchase. It may issue shares up to the nominal amount of the shares it is to purchase. The company can do this because it will have to cancel the shares that it purchases.

2.15   Capital duty that would otherwise be payable under the Finance Act 1973, section 47 (stamp duty on documents relating to chargeable transactions) will be payable only on the amount, if any, by which the actual value of the shares the company issues in place of purchased shares exceeds the value of the shares it purchases at the date of the purchase.

2.16   For this purpose, new shares the company issues before the purchase takes place will be regarded as being issued in place of the purchased shares only if the purchase takes place within one month after their issue. Shares the company issues after the date of purchase may, however, be regarded as being issued in place of the purchased shares to the extent that their nominal value does not exceed the nominal value of the shares the company purchased. This provision is without time limit.

Procedures for purchases

2.17   A private company's purchase of its own shares will be an 'off-market' purchase because either of the following circumstances will apply:

(a)   The shares will not be purchased on a recognised stock exchange.

(b)   The shares will be purchased on a recognised stock exchange but they will not be subject to a marketing arrangement on that stock exchange. In this connection, shares are subject to a marketing arrangement on a recognised stock exchange if either they are listed on that stock exchange or the company has been granted an unrestricted facility for dealings in those shares on that stock exchange (for example, on the Unlisted Securities Market).

Off-market purchases

2.18   A company may make an off-market purchase of its own shares only if it does so under a contract. However, before a company enters into any such contract, the terms of the proposed contract must be authorised by a special resolution of the company. Subsequently, this authority may be varied, or revoked or renewed by a further special resolution. Where there is any proposed variation to an existing contract, there is a similar requirement for a special resolution.

2.19   In determining whether a sufficient number of votes have been cast in favour of the special resolution, it is necessary to disregard the voting rights that attach to the shares that are the subject of the contract. If any member who holds any such shares exercises the voting rights that attach to them, the special resolution will be ineffective unless sufficient other shareholders vote in favour of the resolution. This applies whether the vote is on a poll or on a show of hands. A shareholder whose shares are the subject of the contract (or his proxy), may exercise, on a poll, any voting rights that attach to any other shares in the company that he holds. He may not, however, do so if the voting is on a show of hands.

Any member (or his proxy) may demand a poll on the question of whether the special resolution should be passed. This applies even where, under the articles of association, more than one member is required to demand a poll.

2.20   The special resolution will be effective only if the following documents are made available for inspection:

(a)   The contract, and any variations made to the contract, together with a written memorandum setting out the names of the members who hold the shares to which the contract relates. This memorandum will not be required if those names are set out in the contract itself.

(b)   A written memorandum regarding the terms of the contract if the contract is not in writing. This memorandum must include the names of the members who hold the shares to which the contract relates.

These documents must be available for inspection both at the company's registered office during the 15 days immediately preceding the meeting that will consider the special resolution, and at the meeting itself.

Disclosure of a company's purchase of its own shares

2.21   The company is required to deliver a return to the Registrar of Companies within 28 days of the date on which any shares that it purchased are delivered to it. This return must be in the prescribed form illustrated in Appendix II, and it must state the following:

(a)   The number and the nominal value of each class of shares comprised in the purchase or purchases to which the return relates.

(b)   The date or dates on which the shares were delivered to the company.

Where a company fails to deliver this return to the Registrar of Companies within the specified period, every officer in default is liable to a fine.

2.22   In addition, the company must keep the following documents at its registered office:

(a)   Any contract for the purchase of its own shares.

(b)   Any variation to the terms of any such contract.

If any contract or variation is not in writing, the company must keep a written memorandum of its terms.

The company must keep these documents from the date that the contract was concluded until 10 years have elapsed either from the date that the purchase of all shares under the contract was completed or from the date that the contract terminates. The documents must be available during business hours for members to inspect. They must be available for this purpose without charge and for at least two hours in each day. Subject to this, the company may impose such other reasonable restrictions on the availability of the documents as are approved by an ordinary resolution of the company.

Where a company either does not keep these documents or refuses to allow these documents to be inspected, the company and every officer in default are liable to a fine. Also, the court may order an immediate inspection of the contract or the memorandum in question.

2.23   The directors' report in respect of the year in which the purchases take place must include the following details:

(a)   The number and the nominal value of the shares the company purchased.

(b)   The aggregate consideration the company paid, and the reasons for the purchase.

(c)   The percentage of the called-up share capital that the shares of that description represent.

A company's purchase of its own shares out of capital

2.24   Provided that it satisfies certain conditions, a private company that is entitled under the Companies Act 1981 to purchase its own shares may make a payment towards such a purchase out of capital. A payment made out of capital is a payment otherwise than out of either available distributable profits (as determined under the Companies Act 1980 as amended by the Companies Act 1981) or the proceeds of a new issue of shares. This means that a payment out of capital could include a payment out of unrealised profits.

The conditions that must be satisfied

2.25   A private company may lawfully make a payment out of capital only where it satisfies the conditions set out in paragraphs 2.26 to 2.33. Appendix III contains a checklist that is designed to assist a private company to ensure that it has satisfied all of the relevant conditions.

2.26   The company must be authorised by its articles of association to make a payment out of capital.

2.27   As discussed in paragraphs 2.34 to 2.37, the payment must not exceed the permissible capital payment.

2.28   The directors of the company must make a statutory declaration that both specifies the amount of the permissible capital payment and states that, after enquiring fully into the affairs and the prospects of the company, it is their opinion that both the following apply:

(a)   The company will be able to pay its debts during the period immediately following the date on which it makes the permissible capital payment. When forming this opinion, the directors must take account of all contingent and prospective liabilities that a court would take into account when considering whether the company could pay its debts under the Companies Act 1948, section 222(e) (circumstances in which a company may be wound up by the court). Such contingent and prospective liabilities include, for example, those contingent liabilities that a company is required to disclose in the notes to its annual financial statements and commitments under hire purchase agreements or supply contracts.

(b)   The company will be able to carry on business as a going concern, and will be able to pay its debts as they fall due throughout the year immediately following the date of the proposed payment. When forming this opinion, the directors must consider the plans that they have for the management of the company's business, and also the company's likely liquidity during this year.

The statutory declaration must be in the prescribed form illustrated in Appendix IV. It must contain such information in respect of the nature of the company's business as the Secretary of State may prescribe.

If a director of a company who makes a statutory declaration does not have reasonable grounds for the opinion he has expressed in that declaration, he is liable to either a fine or imprisonment, or both.

2.29   The auditors must make a report that they address to the directors stating that:

(a)   They have enquired into the company's state of affairs.

(b)   The amount specified in the statutory declaration as the permissible capital payment has been properly determined.

(c)   They are not aware of anything that indicates that the directors' expressed opinion is unreasonable in the circumstances.

The directors must attach the auditors' report to the statutory declaration.

2.30   The payment must be approved by a special resolution passed on, or within one week after, the date on which the directors make the statutory declaration.

In determining whether a sufficient number of votes have been cast in favour of the special resolution, it is necessary to disregard the voting rights that attach to the shares to which the resolution relates. If any member who holds any such shares exercises the voting rights that attach to them, the special resolution will be ineffective unless sufficient other shareholders vote in favour of the resolution. This applies whether they vote on a poll or on a show of hands. A shareholder whose shares are the subject of a special resolution may exercise on a poll any voting rights that attach to any other shares that he holds in the company. He may not, however, do so if the voting is on a show of hands.

Even if the articles do not provide for it, any member (or his proxy) may demand a poll on the question of whether the special resolution should be passed.

2.31   The special resolution will be effective only if members can inspect both the statutory declaration and the auditors' report at the meeting at which the resolution is passed. This means that the directors will need to liaise with the company's auditors at an early stage so that the auditors can make their report to the directors before the date of the special resolution.

Where a company refuses to allow a person to inspect the statutory declaration and the auditors' report, the company and every officer in default are liable to a fine. Also, the court may order the company to permit an immediate inspection of the declaration and the report.

2.32   The company must make the payment out of capital not earlier than five weeks, nor later than seven weeks, after the date of the resolution.

2.33   The company must give certain publicity in respect of payments it makes out of capital (as discussed in paragraphs 2.38 to 2.41).

The permissible capital payment.

2.34   Where a payment out of capital is permitted, it must not exceed the amount of the permissible capital payment. For this purpose, the 'permissible capital payment' is the amount by which the price of the purchase exceeds the aggregate of the company's distributable profits and the proceeds of any new issue. The effect of this rule is to require a private company to utilise its available profits and any proceeds arising from a new issue before it makes a payment out of capital. It is only where there is still a deficiency that the company can make a payment out of capital.

If, in the example in Part I of the booklet, Z had purchased Mr. Brown's shares partly out of the proceeds of a new issue of shares, partly out of distributable profits and partly out of capital, this can be illustrated as follows:

In January 1950, Z issued 100,000 ordinary shares of £1 each at a premium of 10p per share. In July 1982, Z has distributable profits of £10,000, and it issues 5,500 ordinary shares of £1 each at a premium of £1 per share for the purposes of purchasing, at a premium of £1.40 per share, Mr. Brown's 10,000 ordinary shares issued in January 1950.

In these circumstances, the permissible capital payment is calculated as follows:

	£
Price of purchase:	
10,000 £1 shares at a premium of £1.40 per share	24,000
Less: Proceeds of issue of 5,500 £1 shares at a premium of	
£1 per share	11,000
Distributable profits	10,000
	21,000
Permissible capital payment	£3,000

2.35   For this purpose, 'distributable profits' has the same meaning as it has in the Companies Act 1980. However, the determination of whether a company has such profit (and if so, its amount) is governed in this case by the Companies Act 1981, section 54, rather than by the Companies Act 1980 section 43.

Under section 54, a company must have reference to the relevant items (as stated in the 'relevant accounts') in order to determine the amount of its permissible capital payment. This requirement is similar to the procedure under the 1980 Act for determining the amount of a company's distributable profits. However, the important difference is that, with a permissible capital payment, the financial statements to which the company must make reference for this purpose are those that are prepared as at any date 'within the period for determining the amount of that payment'. This period is the period of three months that ends with the date on which the directors made the statutory declaration that purported to state the amount of the permissible capital payment. Furthermore, the financial statements must be such as to make it possible to form a *reasonable* (rather than a *proper*) judgement of the amount in question.

2.36   Therefore, it is desirable that the directors should make the statutory declaration within three months of the company's year end. In addition, if the company makes the capital payment at the time that the auditors complete their annual audit, the auditors will normally have sufficient information from their review of post-balance-sheet events and other audit work to make the report to the directors referred to in paragraph 2.29.

2.37   In determining the amount of the permissible capital payment, it is necessary to reduce the amount of distributable profits determined according to the relevant accounts by the amount of any lawful distributions the company made after the date of the relevant accounts and before the date that the directors make their statutory declaration. 'Distributions' for this purpose includes:

(a)   Any financial assistance the company gives for the purpose of acquiring its own or its holding company's shares in circumstances where the Companies Act 1981 requires such payment to be made out of distributable profits.

(b)   Any payment the company makes out of distributable profits in respect of its purchase of any of its own shares.

(c)   Any payment the company makes out of distributable profits in respect of its acquisition of rights to purchase its own shares, or the variation of an existing contract of purchase or the release from any obligation relating to a purchase (as discussed in paragrah 4.07).

Publicity for payments made out of capital.

2.38   The Companies Act 1981 contains provisions that are designed to protect both members and creditors from being unfairly prejudiced by a purchase out of capital. To this end, a company must give certain publicity to the payment within one week of the date on which a special resolution approving the making of a payment out of capital is passed. In particular, the company must publish in the Gazette the following details:

(a)   A statement that the company has approved the making of a payment out of capital for the purpose of purchasing its own shares.

(b)   The amount of the permissible capital payment.

(c)   The date of the resolution.

(d)   A statement that the statutory declaration and the auditors' report are available for inspection at the company's registered office.

(e)   A statement that any creditor of the company may, at any time within five weeks after the date of the resolution, apply to the court for an order that prohibits the payment (as discussed in paragraphs 2.42 to 2.44).

For a company that is registered in England and Wales, the 'Gazette' is the London Gazette. For a company that is registered in Scotland, the 'Gazette' is the Edinburgh Gazette.

2.39   The company must also either publish these details in an appropriate national newspaper or give them in writing to each creditor. For a company that is registered in England and Wales, an 'appropriate national newspaper' is a newspaper that circulates in England and Wales. For a company that is registered in Scotland, an 'appropriate national newspaper' is a newspaper that circulates in Scotland.

2.40   In addition, the company must deliver to the Registrar of Companies a copy of both the statutory declaration and the auditors' report. It must deliver these no later than the date (the 'first notice date') on which the notice referred to in paragraph 2.38 was published either in the Gazette or in the appropriate national newspaper, or was given to each creditor (whichever is earliest).

2.41   Both the statutory declaration and the auditors' report must be open to inspection by any member or any creditor without charge during business hours at the company's registered office. This applies throughout the period that begins with the first notice date and ends five weeks after the date of the resolution.

Where a company refuses to allow these documents to be inspected, the company and every officer in default are liable to a fine. Also, the court may order an immediate inspection of the documents.

Objections by members or creditors.

2.42   After the resolution for making a payment out of capital has been passed, any member or any creditor may, within five weeks from the date of the resolution, apply to the court for the resolution to be cancelled. The application may be made on behalf of either members or creditors by any one or more of them appointed in writing for the purpose. However, the right to object does not extend to any member who consented to, or voted in favour of, the resolution.

2.43   If any application is made to the court for the resolution to be cancelled, the company must take the following action:

(a)   It must immediately give, to the Registrar of Companies, notice in the prescribed form (illustrated in Appendix V) of the application to the court.

(b)   It must, within 15 days of the court making an order (or within such longer period as the court permits), deliver to the Registrar of Companies an office copy of the order.

If the company does not take appropriate action when a member or a creditor makes an application to cancel a resolution for the company to make a payment out of capital, the company and every officer in default are liable to a fine.

2.44   Where an application has been made, the court must make an order that either cancels or confirms the resolution. However, it may do this on such terms and conditions as it thinks fit. In particular, it may:

(a)   Adjourn the proceedings to allow time for an arrangement to be made to the satisfaction of the court for either the purchase of the interests of dissenting members or the protection of dissenting creditors.

(b)   Give such directions and make such orders as it thinks expedient for facilitating or carrying into effect any such arrangement. This may include making an order for the company to purchase the shares and to reduce its share capital, and also to make any consequential amendment to the company's memorandum and articles of association.

(c)   Make an order requiring the company not to make either any alteration at all or any specified alteration to its memorandum or its articles of association. If the court makes such an order, the company has no power, without the court's leave, to make any alteration in breach of that requirement.

(d)   Alter any date or extend any period specified either in the resolution or in any provisions of the Companies Act 1981 regarding the purchase of shares to which the resolution refers.

Civil liability of past shareholders and directors.

2.45   If a company is wound up within a year of making a payment out of capital in respect of a purchase of its shares, and it proves to be insolvent, any shareholder whose shares were purchased, and any director who made the statutory declaration, shall be liable to contribute to the assets of the company to the extent specified in paragraph 2.46. A director will be exempt from such liability, however, if he can show that he had reasonable grounds for forming the opinion stated in the statutory declaration.

2.46   The liability of a past shareholder to contribute to the assets of the company is limited to the amount of the payment the company made out of capital that he received when the company purchased his shares. Where this applies, the company's directors are jointly and severally liable with the past shareholder for that amount. Any person who has contributed an amount to the company's assets under this provision may apply to the court for an order requiring any other person who is jointly and severally liable to reimburse him to the extent that the court considers just and equitable.

2.47   The Companies Act 1948, section 212 (liability as contributories of present and past members) does not apply to a past shareholder's liability in respect of a payment a company made out of capital. Unless the context requires it, a reference to a 'contributory' in a company's articles of association does not include a person who is a contributory only in respect of a payment a company made out of capital. This means that, unless he is a contributory in some other respect, a past shareholder who is liable to contribute in respect of a company's payment out of capital will not be liable, by virtue of section 212, to contribute in any other way.

2.48   A past shareholder who is liable to contribute in respect of a payment a company made out of capital may, by petition, apply to the court for the winding up of the company on the following grounds:

(a)   The company is unable to pay its debts.

(b)   It is just and equitable for the company to be wound up.

In these circumstances, the Companies Act 1948, section 224(1)(a) (restriction on the right of a contributory to present a petition) does not apply. However, unless a past shareholder is a contributory not only in respect of a company's payment out of capital, but also in other respects, he may not petition the court for the winding up of the company on other grounds.

Maintenance of capital

2.49   To safeguard creditors by ensuring that a company's capital is maintained except where it purchases its own shares out of capital, the Companies Act 1981 requires it to make a transfer to the capital redemption reserve in certain circumstances. The 1981 Act also contains provisions that enable a private company to utilise its capital redemption reserve when it purchases its own shares in certain circumstances.

Transfers to capital redemption reserve.

2.50   Where a company purchases its own shares wholly out of distributable profits, it must transfer to the capital redemption reserve an amount equivalent to the nominal value of the shares it purchased.

2.51   Where a company purchases its own shares wholly or partly out of the proceeds of a new issue (but without making any payment out of capital), it must transfer to the capital redemption reserve the amount, if any, by which the nominal value of the shares it purchased exceeds the aggregate proceeds from the new issue.

2.52   Where a company purchases its own shares wholly or partly by making a payment out of capital (but without applying the proceeds of any new issue), it must transfer to the capital redemption reserve the amount, if any, by which the nominal value of the shares it purchased exceeds the payment out of capital.

2.53   Where a company purchases its own shares by a payment that includes both the proceeds of a new issue of shares and a payment out of capital, it must transfer to the capital redemption reserve the amount, if any, by which the nominal value of the shares it purchased exceeds the aggregate of the proceeds and the payment the company made out of capital.

2.54   The following example illustrates these provisions:

Companies A, B, C and D (all private companies) each purchase 10,000 of their own shares that were originally issued at their nominal value of £1 per share. In each case, a premium of £1.40 per share is payable on purchase. The purchases are to be made as follows:

	A £	B £	C £	D £
Out of proceeds of new issue of shares at nominal value	—	7,000	—	4,000
Out of distributable profits	24,000	17,000	16,000	15,000
Out of capital	—	—	8,000	5,000
	£24,000	£24,000	£24,000	£24,000

In these circumstances, the amount that each company must transfer to its capital redemption reserve is as follows:

	A £	B £	C £	D £
Nominal value of shares purchased	10,000	10,000	10,000	10,000
Less: Proceeds of new issue	—	7,000	—	4,000
Payment out of capital			8,000	5,000
	—	7,000	8,000	9,000
Transfer to capital redemption reserve	£10,000	£3,000	£2,000	£1,000

The effect on the summarised balance sheets can be illustrated as follows:

	A £	B £	C £	D £
Before purchase				
Share capital	100,000	100,000	100,000	100,000
Distributable reserves	50,000	30,000	16,000	15,000
	£150,000	£130,000	£116,000	£115,000
Net assets other than cash	125,000	105,000	90,000	80,000
Cash	25,000	25,000	26,000	35,000
	£150,000	£130,000	£116,000	£115,000

After purchase	A £	B £	C £	D £
Share capital	90,000	97,000	90,000	94,000
Capital redemption reserve	10,000	3,000	2,000	1,000
	100,000	100,000	92,000	95,000
Distributable reserves	26,000	13,000	—	—
	£126,000	£113,000	£92,000	£95,000
Net assets other than cash	125,000	105,000	90,000	80,000
Cash	1,000	8,000	2,000	15,000
	£126,000	£113,000	£92,000	£95,000

Utilisation of the capital redemption reserve when a private company purchases its own shares.

2.55 Where there are no proceeds from a new issue, and the company's payment out of capital exceeds the nominal value of the shares it purchased, the company may reduce one or more of the following by amounts that in aggregate do not exceed the excess:

(a)   The capital redemption reserve.

(b)   The share premium account.

(c)   The fully-paid share capital.

(d)   The credit balance on the revaluation reserve set up to comply with the alternative accounting rules in the Companies Act 1948, new Schedule 8.

2.56 Where there are proceeds from a new issue, as well as a payment out of capital, the aggregate amount by which (a) to (d) in paragraph 2.55 can be reduced is the amount by which the aggregate of the proceeds of a new issue and any payment out of capital exceeds the nominal value of the shares the company purchased.

2.57 The following example illustrates these provisions:

Companies E, F and G (all private companies) purchase 10,000 of their own shares that were originally issued at a premium of 10p per share. The nominal value of the shares in question is £1 per share and, in each case, a premium of £1.40 per share is payable. The purchases are to be made as follows:

	E £	F £	G £
Out of distributable profits	12,000	10,000	13,000
Out of proceeds of new issue of shares at nominal value	—	4,000	11,000
Out of capital	12,000	10,000	—
	£24,000	£24,000	£24,000

In these circumstances, the aggregate amount by which each company may reduce the capital redemption reserve, the share premium account, the fully-paid share capital and the credit balance on the revaluation reserve is as follows:

	E	*F*	*G*
	£	£	£
Nominal value of shares purchased	10,000	10,000	10,000
Proceeds of new issue	—	4,000	11,000
Payment out of capital	12,000	10,000	—
	12,000	14,000	11,000
Excess available	£2,000	£4,000	Nil

Note: Although the proceeds of the new issue by G exceed the nominal value of the shares purchased, G may not utilise the 'excess' in the manner envisaged by paragraph 2.56 because G did not make a payment out of capital.

If companies E and F use the excess available solely to reduce the capital redemption reserve, the effect on the summarised balance sheets can be illustrated as follows:

	E	*F*
	£	£
Before purchase		
Share capital	100,000	100,000
Capital redemption reserve	3,000	6,000
	103,000	106,000
Distributable reserves	12,000	10,000
	£115,000	£116,000
Net assets other than cash	90,000	80,000
Cash	25,000	36,000
	£115,000	£116,000
After purchase		
Share capital	90,000	94,000
Capital redemption reserve	1,000	2,000
	£91,000	£96,000
Net assets other than cash	90,000	80,000
Cash	1,000	16,000
	£91,000	£96,000

2.58 The power to reduce (a) to (d) in paragraph 2.55 is permissive and not mandatory. Consequently, a private company need not make such a reduction at all. Alternatively, it may make only a partial reduction.

A company's failure to purchase shares

2.59   Where a company has agreed on or after 15 June 1982 to purchase any of its shares, and then fails to purchase them in accordance with the agreement, the shareholder affected may not sue the company for damages. This restriction on the shareholder's rights is without prejudice to any other rights that the shareholder has under the law (for example, the right to apply for an order of specific performance). However, if a company shows in such circumstances that it has insufficient distributable profits to meet the cost of purchasing the shares, the court may not grant an order of specific performance of the terms of purchase.

The effect of a winding up on a company's obligation to purchase shares

2.60   In addition to the provisions discussed in paragraph 2.59, the Companies Act 1981 contains provisions that apply where a company is wound up and where it has agreed on or after 15 June 1982 to purchase shares, but it has not purchased those shares at the time that the winding up commences.

In such circumstances, the court may generally enforce the terms of the purchase against the company. Where the court does this, the company must cancel the shares in question. Any liability that arises on a winding up from a company's failure to fulfil an obligation to purchase its shares may be satisfied only when:

(a)   All other debts and liabilities (including any interest deferred under the Bankruptcy Act 1914, section 66) have been paid. This will not apply where the debts or the liabilities in question are due to members by virtue only of the fact that they are members.

(b)   All rights attached to those shares that have priority have been satisfied.

However, the liability must be paid in preference to all other members' rights (whether as to capital or income).

The terms of the purchase will not be enforceable in this way, however, where either of the following applies:

(a)   The terms provide for the purchase to take place at a date later than the date on which the winding up commenced.

(b)   The company was unable (during the period between the date specified for the purchase to take place and the date that the winding up commenced) to make a lawful distribution equal in amount to the purchase price.

Powers of the Secretary of State

2.61   The power of a company to purchase its own shares represents a fundamental change in UK company law. Because of this, it is impossible to know in advance all the circumstances in which companies will exercise this new power, or the precise effect it will have on members and creditors when companies do so. Consequently, the Government was anxious that it should be able to make any necessary modifications without needing to pass a further Companies Act. Accordingly, the Secretary of State may modify by statutory instrument the 1981 Act provisions that relate to:

(a)   The authority required for a company to purchase any of its own shares.

(b)   The authority a company requires for the release of its rights under any contract for the purchase of its own shares.

(c)   The information a company must include in the return it has to deliver to the Registrar of Companies (as referred to in paragraph 2.21).

(d)   The payment of premiums on purchase out of share premium account.

(e)   The directors' statutory declaration required when a company proposes to make a payment out of capital.

(f)   The contents of the auditors' report required to be attached to the directors' statutory declaration.

(g)   The inclusion of distributable profits in the calculation of the permissible capital payment.

In particular, he may make different provisions for different cases or classes of case. He may also make such further consequential, incidental and supplementary provisions as he thinks fit.

THE TAX LAW PROVISIONS

2.62   The provisions in the Finance Act 1982 that make it advantageous for an unquoted company to purchase its own shares in certain circumstances are explained by reference to the simple example given in Part I of the booklet. Accordingly, the assumptions of that example are repeated below.

Z Limited (Z) (a private, unquoted company) is a long-established family manufacturing company. Mr. Brown (a director of Z) purchased for £10,000 many years ago 10,000 of Z's 100,000 issued ordinary £1 shares. He has now had a major disagreement with his fellow directors about the way in which Z is run. The directors and the other shareholders have agreed that it is in everyone's best interests for Mr. Brown to sever his links with the company. He will resign as a director, and the company will purchase his shares from him for £24,000 (which is the agreed market value). The company will make the payment out of distributable profits.

The qualifying conditions

2.63   The five qualifying conditions that a company must satisfy before the favourable tax treatment applies are set out in paragraphs 2.64 to 2.68. An explanation of how these qualifying conditions are modified in special circumstances is set out in paragraphs 2.70 to 2.82.

2.64   First, the company that is buying its own shares must be an *unquoted trading company*.

A company is unquoted unless either it has a class of shares listed in the official list of a stock exchange or it is the subsidiary of such a company. In the example above, Z was a family company. If none of its shares were listed on a stock exchange (as would be likely if members of the family owned all the shares), then Z would qualify as an unquoted company.

In tax law, 'trade' has a specialised meaning. Z would qualify as a trading company because it carries on a manufacturing business. Similarly, wholesaling and retailing companies would be trading companies. However, businesses such as investment companies would not qualify as trading companies. In addition, the new legislation specifically excludes certain trades from the benefits of the favourable tax treatment. The excluded trades are those of dealing in shares, or securities, or land or commodity futures. These exclusions are unlikely to be of any great impact in practice. Moreover, for a company to qualify as a trading company it is not sufficient that it should carry on a trade if it also has activities that are not trading activities. For a company to qualify for relief under the new rules, its business must consist wholly or mainly of the carrying on of a trade or trades.

2.65   Second, the legislation can apply only if the purpose behind the company's purchase of its own shares is to *benefit its trade*. At first sight, it may appear difficult to say that it is to the benefit of a company's trade for the company to purchase its own shares and thereby deplete its bank balance or increase its overdraft. However, it appears that the legislation is looking for a good commercial reason that will outweigh this temporary depletion, and be of substantial longer-term benefit. The removal of a dissentient director shareholder, as in the example, might be sufficient reason. Another sufficient reason might be, for example, where a competitor acquired shares in the company, and then tried to use his shareholding to advance his own trading position at the company's expense.

Conversely, there are occasions when the new legislation will not apply. For example, the favourable tax treatment will be denied if the shareholders try to use the legislation to enjoy the profits of the company without the company paying a dividend. Similarly, if the company's purchase of its own shares is part of a tax avoidance arrangement, the new legislation will not apply.

Broadly speaking, therefore, if this second qualifying condition is to be satisfied, there must be a good commercial reason behind the purchase. This test could cause uncertainties in practice. Consequently, the Inland Revenue have issued a statement of practice on their interpretation of the 'benefit of the trade' test. The Inland Revenue's view is not law, but it is useful to know the circumstances in which they will apply the new rules.

The Inland Revenue say that the test requires that the sole or main purpose of the company's purchase of its own shares should be to benefit the company's trade. It should not be intended to benefit the shareholder who is selling, although there will, of course, be an incidental benefit to him. Nor will it be sufficient that a shareholder wishes to extract funds from a company and then to apply them for some other commercial purpose.

The Inland Revenue say that the new rules will probably apply where the shareholder is genuinely giving up his entire interest of all kinds in the company. This might arise where there is a board room disagreement as in the example given above. Other examples that the Inland Revenue say should normally qualify are as follows:

(a) An outside shareholder has provided equity finance and is now withdrawing his investment.

(b) The proprietor of a company is retiring to make way for new management.

(c) A shareholder has died leaving shares in his estate, and his personal representatives or the beneficiaries do not wish to keep them.

It is not necessary for a shareholder to sell *all* of his shares. The new tax rules can apply if he substantially reduces his shareholding (as discussed in paragraph 2.68). However, if a shareholder retains some shares in the company this might mean that the benefit of the trade test is not satisfied. For example, if he retained some shares, it could not be argued that the purpose of the company's purchase was to remove the shareholder's influence. However, there are circumstances in which the test is satisfied even though the shareholder does not sell all of his shares. For example, he may wish to retain a few shares for sentimental reasons. Provided that the requirement of a substantial reduction in his holding is satisfied, then the new tax treatment could apply. Alternatively, the company might not be able to afford to purchase all of a particular shareholder's shares at one time. If there was an arrangement that the company would purchase all of his shares over a period, with the intention that he should ultimately leave the company completely, then it appears that the test would be satisfied.

It should be noted that the Inland Revenue's views are not the law. They merely represent circumstances in which the Inland Revenue believe the new legislation will apply.

The Inland Revenue's views are, of course, very useful guidance for shareholders about the way in which the new legislation applies. But if a company has a genuine commercial reason for purchasing some of its own shares, then it should not be deterred from seeking the benefits of the new tax legislation merely because its reason does not fall within the precise terms of the Inland Revenue's statement. An application for an advance clearance should be made.

2.66 Third, before Mr. Brown can enjoy the favourable tax treatment, he must show that he is both *resident and ordinarily resident* within the UK for tax purposes. The expressions 'resident' and 'ordinarily resident' are concepts of general tax law. Broadly speaking, Mr. Brown would normally satisfy this condition if he habitually lives in the UK.

The same rule applies where the shareholder is not an individual, but is a company or the trustees of a settlement. In addition, if a nominee holds any shares, then the nominee, too, must be resident and ordinarily resident in the UK.

The reasons for this condition are straightforward. If the shareholder was not resident in the UK, he would not even be liable to capital gains tax when the company purchases his shares. The Inland Revenue doubtless considered this a little too generous, and so they imposed the residence requirement to ensure that some tax would be collected. In addition, the Inland Revenue believe it would be too difficult to police the new legislation unless all parties involved are UK-resident.

2.67   Fourth, in the example, Mr. Brown acquired the shares many years ago. To qualify under the new legislation, he would have to demonstrate that he had owned the shares for at least *five years* up to the date on which the company purchased his shares.

2.68   Fifth, in the example, the company purchased all of Mr. Brown's shares. Accordingly, he would meet this qualifying condition. However, the company does not need to purchase all of a particular shareholder's shares, provided that his shareholding is *substantially reduced*. Broadly speaking, provided that Z acquired more than one-quarter of Mr. Brown's shares, the favourable tax treatment would apply. The precise rules for ascertaining whether there has been a substantial reduction in the shareholding are explained in paragraph 2.70.

Special circumstances

2.69   In practice, it is unlikely that the facts will be as straightforward as the assumptions of the example. To take account of the complexities that will probably be met in practice, the terms of the qualifying conditions are modified accordingly. These modifications are explained in the following paragraphs.

Substantial reduction in shareholding.

2.70   In the simple example, the company purchased all of Mr. Brown's shares. However, the company does not need to purchase all of Mr. Brown's shares for the favourable tax treatment to apply.

Suppose that Z had 10,000 shares in issue, each worth (say) £20, giving a total capital value of £200,000. Suppose also that Mr. Brown owns 60 per cent of the share capital (that is, he owns 6,000 shares), and that the remaining shares are owned by directors unrelated to Mr. Brown. Z has been experiencing trading difficulties. An outside investor agrees to inject £150,000 by way of share capital to assist the company. However, this investor insists that his investment should give him a majority interest in the company.

If, of course, the investor merely subscribes his £150,000 for shares at their value of £20 each, he would obtain only 7,500 shares out of a total share capital of 17,500 — which is not a majority interest. Accordingly, Mr. Brown agrees that he will sell 3,000 shares to the company before the outside investor subscribes his £150,000.

To determine whether the substantial reduction requirement is satisfied, two tests have to be met.

The first test comprises the following:

(a)   Calculate the percentage of the issued shares Mr. Brown owned before the sale. This was 60 per cent, that is 6,000 shares out of 10,000.

(b)   Calculate the same percentage after the sale. This would be approximately 43 per cent, that is 3,000 shares out of 7,000.

(c)   The after-sale percentage must be less than threequarters of the pre-sale percentage. Threequarters of 60 per cent is 45 per cent. Because 43 per cent is less than 45 per cent, the first test is satisfied.

The second test is that, after the sale, the shareholder must not have an interest (directly or indirectly) of more than 30 per cent in the company's share capital. As just explained, after the sale Mr. Brown owned 43 per cent of the issued share capital of the company. Accordingly, he would not satisfy the second test, and the favourable tax treatment would not be available.

2.71   One way in which Mr. Brown might overcome the difficulty mentioned above, and qualify for favourable tax treatment, would be if the outside investor subscribed his £150,000 for shares *before* Mr. Brown sold his 3,000 shares to the company. If the transactions were carried out in this sequence then, immediately after the sale to the company, Mr. Brown would hold 3,000 shares out of a total issued share capital of 14,500 shares. This would be well below the 30 per cent mark. However, it is not yet known whether this suggested solution would be challenged by the Inland Revenue.

2.72   The one-quarter reduction test (the first test above) applies not only to the shareholder's holding but also to his participation in profits. This caters, for example, for companies that either have several classes of share capital or have loan stocks that carry a right to participation in profits.

2.73   Provision is also made for companies that have classes of shares that carry different voting rights. After the sale, the shareholder must not have more than 30 per cent of the voting power in the company.

Substantial reduction in shareholding where shareholder has associates.

2.74   In the example in paragraph 2.70, Mr. Brown held shares in Z, and unrelated individuals held the remaining shares in the company. However, it might be that, perhaps for tax-planning reasons, Mr. Brown had previously transferred some shares to his wife, or perhaps to a trust for their children. In these circumstances, a further provision determines whether there has been a substantial reduction in Mr. Brown's shareholding.

The approach taken is to combine the shareholdings of Mr. Brown, his wife and the trustees, and regard them as one shareholding in deciding whether there has been a substantial reduction. The rules explained above for determining whether there has been a substantial reduction are then applied to the combined shareholding.

The rules about associates are complicated, but the most important categories of persons regarded as associates are as follows:

(a)   A husband and wife living together.

(b)   Parents and their minor children.

(c)   A person who has more than 30 per cent in a company and that company, and any other company which that company controls.

(d)   Companies under common control.

(e)   Settlors and trustees.

Whenever a shareholder has associates, his shareholding is tested under the substantial reduction rules. To determine whether the shareholder qualifies under the new rules, the test is carried out both on his shareholding alone and on his shareholding taken together with the shareholdings of all his associates.

2.75 It may happen that, where a company wishes to purchase its own shares from a vendor, the new relief will apply only if associates of the vendor also sell shares that they own to the company. If these circumstances apply, and if, in order to enable the vendor to qualify for the new relief one of his associates agrees to sell some of his shares, then the associate will qualify for relief. This applies even though his interest may not be substantially reduced, provided that the other requirements are satisfied. If, however, the associate sells a greater number of shares than are required to enable the vendor to qualify for relief, the associate will not qualify for relief in respect of the shares in excess of that number (unless his own shareholding is, in fact, substantially reduced).

Shares that are inherited.

2.76 One of the basic qualifying conditions is that the shares should be owned for at least five years up to the date of sale. For this purpose, the period of ownership by the deceased, the personal representatives and the vendor are combined. Where shares are sold to the company by personal representatives or a beneficiary under a will, the five-year period is reduced to three years. This means that if the total exceeds three years, the qualifying condition is satisfied.

The rule applies where shares are either inherited from an estate or sold to the company by the personal representative. If the shares are received from, say, a family trust, the condition would be satisfied only if the recipient has owned the shares for five years. This is so even if he was the sole beneficiary of the trust.

Shares that are transferred between spouses.

2.77 Where shares are transferred between spouses, the period of ownership of both will count towards the five-year period of ownership. This does not apply, however, if the donor spouse is alive but no longer living with the donee.

Rules for identifying acquisitions and disposals.

2.78 For the purpose of determining whether the five-year ownership test is satisfied, the rules for identifying acquisitions and disposals have been drafted in the most favourable way for the shareholder. Shares that were acquired earlier are taken into account before shares that were acquired later. Previous disposals are treated as having been made out of shares acquired later rather than earlier.

2.79 In the example in paragraph 2.62, Mr. Brown acquired all of his shares at one time many years ago. If, instead, he had acquired 5,000 shares ten years ago and 5,000 shares three years ago, the five-year test would not be satisfied on a purchase of all his shares. Consequently, the whole of the gain would be charged to income tax.

It would seem to be possible, however, to utilise the rule to overcome this disadvantage. There appears to be no reason why the company should not effect the purchase in two stages. The first stage would be to purchase the shares the shareholder acquired ten years ago. The gain on this purchase would be charged to capital gains tax. The second stage would be to purchase the shares the shareholder acquired three years ago. The gain on this purchase would be charged to income tax. Although part of the gain would be charged to income tax, the gain on the shares the shareholder acquired more than five years ago would be charged only to capital gains tax. This treatment is surely within the spirit of the rules. This example merely serves to illustrate the principle that there is no equity in a tax statute, although the taxpayer's professional advisers may be alert enough to plan a transaction in such a way as to achieve an equitable result.

Shares in a holding company.

2.80 Many businesses are carried on through groups of companies whose shares are held by a holding company. Such a company is sometimes treated as an investment company. As already explained, an investment company does not, for tax purposes, carry on a trade. Consequently, it could not satisfy one of the basic qualifying conditions. However, because the structure just mentioned is so common, the basic condition is relaxed to enable such companies to qualify under the new rules. The condition is satisfied if the business of the group of companies looked at together, consists wholly or mainly of trading activities.

For this purpose, a group consists of all companies in the UK and overseas in which the holding company has a 75 per cent interest, which it holds either directly or indirectly.

Shareholdings in different companies in the same group.

2.81 The straightforward test for a substantial reduction in a shareholding is inappropriate where shares are held in different companies in the same group. For this purpose, a group means a company and its 51 per cent subsidiaries, provided that the company is not itself a 51 per cent subsidiary. The test is modified in the way discussed below.

The shareholdings in each company before the sale are calculated as a fraction of each company's issued share capital. The fractions are totalled and divided by the number of 'relevant companies' in the group. A relevant company is one in which the vendor owns shares either immediately before or immediately after the sale. The same procedure is carried out after the sale. The two average shareholdings are compared to determine whether there has been a substantial reduction. Broadly similar rules apply for establishing a substantial reduction in the participation in the profits of a group.

If there are associates, their shareholdings are included in the calculation.

The following example illustrates the effect of the rules:

A group consists of three companies, Z and its two subsidiaries X and Y. The share capital and the parts Mr. Brown holds are as follows:

	Share capital	*Shares owned by Mr. Brown*	*Percentage shareholding*
	£		%
Z	10,000	1,000	10
X	10,000	500	5
Y	10,000	Nil	-
			15

The shareholding test.

To determine Mr. Brown's interest in the group before the sale, his total 15 per cent interest is divided by the number of relevant companies (namely, two). Therefore, his interest is, for this purpose, 7.5 per cent. (Y is not a relevant company because Mr. Brown does not hold any shares in it.)

Mr. Brown sells 500 of his shares in Z to that company for £4,000. Thereafter, he holds 500 shares out of the 9,500 shares in issue. After the sale his interest in the relevant companies in the group is therefore:

Z	5.26%
X	5.00%
Y	—
	10.26%

When this figure is divided by 2 as before, Mr. Brown's interest is shown to be 5.13 per cent.

His shareholding has been reduced by 2.37 per cent, which exceeds one-quarter of 7.5 per cent.

Mr. Brown will also satisfy the 30 per cent test because his holding in Z is only 5.26 per cent, and his holding in X (both directly and indirectly) is 5 per cent plus 5.26 per cent of 95 per cent = 5.54 per cent. His total holding, therefore, is 10.54 per cent.

The profit participation test.

The reduction of profit participation is as shown below. Whilst there may be other special additions to profits, the only one applicable in this case is a special addition of £100 for each company.

Before sale	Z	X	Y
Profits (including special addition)	£20,100	£50,100	£20,100
Deemed distributions by:			
X to Z (95%)	47,595		
Y to Z (100%)	20,100		
	£87,795		
Shareholding of			
Mr. Brown	10%	5%	Nil
Share of profits	£8,779	£2,505	
After sale			
Profits, less amount paid for shares	£16,100	£50,100	£20,100
Deemed distributions by:			
X to Z	47,595		
Y to Z	20,100		
	£83,795		
Shareholding of			
Mr. Brown	5.26%	5%	Nil
Share of profits	£4,407	£2,505	

The profit participation is reduced from £11,284 (that is, £8,779 plus £2,505) to £6,912 (that is, £4,407 plus £2,505). This is clearly less than 75 per cent of the original share of profits.

2.82 In certain circumstances, other companies may be included in the group. In order to obtain the benefit of the new rules, a profitable company could be taken out of the group for a period of time. In order to counteract this device, such a company will be treated as continuing to be a member of the group if there are arrangements under which it could again become a member of the group. Similarly, where the whole, or a significant part, of the business carried out by an unquoted company is transferred to a second company, that second company, and any company of which it is a 51 per cent subsidiary, will be treated as members of the same group as the company that previously carried on that business. This treatment will, however, apply only if the transfer of the whole or part of the business occurred within the three years before a company purchased its own shares. These rules may bring the group rules into play even where the company that is purchasing its own shares is not otherwise a member of a group.

The qualifying conditions where a company's purchase of its own shares is to enable a capital transfer tax liability to be paid

2.83 It often happens that an individual will spend his working life building up his family company so that on his death the bulk of the value of his estate is represented by his shareholding in the company. This situation can cause particular problems where there are insufficient liquid assets with which to meet the capital transfer tax (CTT) liability that arises when the shareholder dies. This problem has long been recognised as a particular one with family companies. Various attempts have been made to lessen the impact of CTT (for example, the special business property relief from CTT). Provided that all three of the conditions set out below are satisfied, the new tax rules will apply where a company purchases its own shares to enable CTT on a death to be paid:

(a)   The company is an unquoted trading company. This is the same requirement as the first basic qualifying condition explained in paragraph 2.64.

(b)   The recipient uses the whole, or substantially the whole, of the proceeds of sale to meet a CTT liability that arises when the shareholder dies. In practice, it will be possible to meet this condition if the company simply buys sufficient shares to put the executors in funds to meet the CTT liability. The liability must, however, be met within two years of the shareholder's death. Any capital gains tax payable in these circumstances will not prejudice the conclusion as to whether substantially the whole of the proceeds have been applied in payment of the CTT liability.

(c)   Undue hardship would otherwise occur. Unfortunately, the legislation gives no definition of 'undue hardship'. Each case will have to be considered on its own facts.

2.84   Two further important points need to be noted.

First, the three conditions set out in the preceding paragraph are the *only* conditions to be satisfied for the new tax rules to apply. The other qualifying conditions do not apply in these circumstances.

Second, if the three conditions *are* satisfied, any gain on the shares over their original cost is treated as a capital gain. However, the capital gains tax legislation contains a special provision that means that capital gains that arise on death are not taxable. Only the increase in value after death is taxable.

2.85   This special application of the provisions where a company's purchase of its own shares is essential to meet a CTT liability is a welcome innovation. It should reduce the fears of entrepreneurs about the break-up of their family companies when they die.

Applications to the Inland Revenue for advance clearance

2.86   If a company purchased its own shares under the impression that the purchase was within the new legislation, and subsequently discovered it was not, the consequences would clearly be unpleasant.

Accordingly, provision is made for a company to obtain advance clearance for such a purchase.

2.87   The company should make an application to the Inland Revenue for clearance. The application should contain written details of the proposed transaction. Appendix VI comprises the guidance that the Inland Revenue have issued on the content of applications for clearance. The Inland Revenue are obliged to say, within 30 days, whether the proposed transaction falls within the new rules. Should the Inland Revenue require any further information, the 30-day time limit begins from the time that they receive that information. Of course, if an advance clearance application did not contain full details of any proposed transaction, then any clearance the Inland Revenue gave would not bind them.

2.88   Conversely, investors (notably institutions) sometimes prefer that when they sell their shares to the company this should be treated as a dividend. The company can apply in advance for confirmation that the new rules will not apply.

Return of the purchase to the Inland Revenue

2.89   If a company buys its own shares, and considers that the new rules apply to the purchase, it is required to make a return of the purchase to the Inland Revenue. It must make the return within 60 days of the date of the purchase. The return must contain details of the payment the company made, and the circumstances that bring the purchase within the new rules.

2.90   Any person who, with his associates, has more than a 30 per cent interest in the company, is required to give notice to the inspector of any scheme or arrangement that would prevent the rules applying.

The person must give the notice within 60 days after he first knows of the payment and of the scheme or arrangement.

Enquiries the inspector is empowered to make

2.91   The inspector is empowered to make enquiries where he believes a company's purchase of its own shares was part of a tax avoidance arrangement. The inspector may make enquiries only of the purchasing company, or of any person that has an interest, together with the interests of his associates, of 30 per cent or more in the company. The enquiries are limited to information which that company or person can reasonably obtain.

Part III: Public companies

This part contains an explanation of the different provisions of company law and tax law that apply when either a public, unquoted company or a public, quoted company purchases its own shares.

THE COMPANY LAW PROVISIONS

3.01 Subject to certain conditions, any public company that has a share capital may purchase any of its own shares. This applies whether or not the shares in question are redeemable. If it satisfies the conditions, a public company may purchase its own shares in accordance with the procedures described in this part of the booklet.

The conditions that must be satisfied

3.02 The conditions that a public company must satisfy before it can purchase its own shares are, with one exception, the same as those for a private company as set out in paragraphs 2.03 to 2.09 and 2.11 to 2.13.

3.03 The one exception is that a public company may not purchase its own shares out of capital. A public company must make the purchase either out of distributable profits or out of the proceeds of a new issue of shares it makes for the purposes of the purchase.

3.04 In addition, however, as compared with a private company a public company that wishes to purchase its own shares must satisfy one additional condition. That additional condition is that it must, after the purchase, satisfy the requirements of the Companies Act 1980 in respect of its allotted share capital. In particular, its allotted share capital after the purchase must not be less than the authorised minimum (which is currently £50,000).

3.05 The company must follow the detailed procedure that the Companies Act 1981 specifies (as discussed in paragraphs 3.07 to 3.14).

The issue of shares for the purposes of a purchase

3.06 The conditions that apply to a private company (as discussed in paragraphs 2.14 to 2.16) apply also to a public company.

Procedures for purchases

3.07 A public company's purchase of its own shares may be either an 'off-market' purchase or a 'market' purchase.

A purchase is an 'off-market' purchase in either of the following circumstances:

(a)   The shares are not purchased on a recognised stock exchange.

(b)   The shares are purchased on a recognised stock exchange, but they are *not* subject to a marketing arrangement on that stock exchange. In this connection, shares are subject to a marketing arrangement on a recognised stock exchange if either they are listed on that stock exchange or the company has been granted an unrestricted facility for dealings in those shares on that stock exchange (for example, on the Unlisted Securities Market).

A purchase is a 'market' purchase if it is a purchase of shares that are subject to a marketing arrangement on a recognised stock exchange. It includes, therefore, a purchase of shares on the Unlisted Securities Market.

Off-market purchases.

3.08 The procedures for an off-market purchase by a public company are the same as those for a private company as set out in paragraphs 2.18 to 2.20. A public company, however, has to satisfy one additional requirement.

3.09 The additional requirement for a public company is that the authority given it by the special resolution must also specify the date on which the authority expires. This date must be no later than 18 months from the date on which the special resolution is passed.

Market purchases.

3.10 A company may make a market purchase only if the purchase is first authorised by the company in general meeting. Only an ordinary resolution is required.

3.11 To comply with the Companies Act 1981, the authority to purchase the shares *must*:

(a)   Specify the maximum number of shares the company may acquire.

(b)   Determine both the maximum and the minimum prices that the company may pay for the shares that it is authorised to purchase. For this purpose, the authority may either specify a particular sum or provide a basis or a formula for calculating the amount in question. Where the latter applies, however, the basis or the formula must be determined by reference to objective criteria, rather than by reference to any person's opinion or discretion. This requirement to state both the maximum and the minimum prices that the company may pay for the shares may cause problems if the authority is to be effective under volatile stock market conditions.

(c)   Specify the date on which the authority expires. The maximum period for which the authority may last is 18 months from the date on which the resolution was passed. However, a company may purchase its own shares after the authority has expired provided that:

(i)   The contract of purchase was concluded before the authority expired.

(ii)   The terms of the authority permitted the company to enter into a contract that might be executed only after the authority expired.

3.12   In addition, the authority *may*:

(a)   Be either a general authority to purchase the company's shares or an authority limited to the purchase of shares of any particular class or description. (Thus, the authority to purchase may be limited to a particular holding.)

(b)   Impose conditions.

(c)   Be varied, or revoked or renewed by a subsequent ordinary resolution.

3.13   Within 15 days of the passing of any resolution that relates to a company's authority to purchase its own shares, the company must send to the Registrar of Companies a printed copy of the resolution.

3.14   Two important differences exist between the authority for an off-market purchase and the authority for a market purchase. With an off-market purchase, a specific contract of purchase must be approved and it must be approved by special resolution. With a market purchase, the authority that requires approval is an authority to purchase shares. This authority need not relate to any particular shares, and it need be approved only by an ordinary resolution.

Disclosure of a company's purchase of its own shares

3.15   The disclosure requirements for a public company's purchase of its own shares are the same as those for a private company as set out in paragraphs 2.21 to 2.23. However, a public company has to satisfy two additional requirements.

3.16   The first additional requirement relates to the return that the company must deliver to the Registrar of Companies (as discussed in paragraph 2.21).

The return that a public company has to deliver must also state the following:

(a)   The aggregate amount that the company paid for all the shares covered by the return.

(b)   The maximum and the minimum prices that the company paid in respect of each class of shares comprised in the purchase or purchases to which the return relates.

3.17   The second additional requirement relates to the inspection of the documents referred to in paragraph 2.22.

The documents must be available for inspection both by members *and* by any other person.

Maintenance of capital

3.18 To safeguard creditors by ensuring that a public company's capital is maintained whenever it purchases its own shares, the Companies Act 1981 requires the company to make transfers to its capital redemption reserve in the circumstances set out in paragraphs 2.50 and 2.51.

A company's failure to purchase shares

3.19 The conditions that apply to a private company that are discussed in paragraph 2.59 apply also to a public company.

The effect of a winding up on a company's obligation to purchase shares

3.20 The provisions of the Companies Act 1981 (discussed in paragraph 2.60) that apply to a private company apply also to a public company.

Powers of the Secretary of State

3.21 The Secretary of State's powers that apply to a private company, and that are discussed in paragraph 2.61, apply also to a public company.

THE TAX LAW PROVISIONS

3.22 The tax law provisions that apply to a public company's purchase of its own shares will depend on whether the company is an unquoted, public company or a quoted, public company.

Provisions that apply to an unquoted, public company

3.23 The new tax rules will apply to an unquoted, public company's purchase of its own shares provided that the company satisfies all of the qualifying conditions explained in Part II of this booklet.

3.24 Shares that do not have a full stock exchange quotation, but are listed on the Unlisted Securities Market, are regarded as unquoted for the purposes of the new rules. Thus, a company that has its shares listed on the Unlisted Securities Market has the advantage of a market for its shares without the disadvantage of an official listing.

Provisions that apply to a quoted, public company

3.25 The new tax rules will not apply to a quoted, public company's purchase of its own shares. The normal rules that treat the payment as a distribution will automatically apply.

3.26 A public company will be quoted either if it has a class of shares listed in the official list of a stock exchange or if it is the subsidiary of such a company.

Part IV

This part contains an explanation of:

1. Contingent purchase contracts.

2. The assignment or the release of a company's right to purchase its own shares.

3. Payments for transactions other than purchases.

4. The requirements of the City Code on Take-overs and Mergers.

5. The requirements of The Stock Exchange.

Contingent purchase contracts

4.01 A contingent purchase contract is a contract under which a company may (subject to any conditions) become either entitled or obliged to purchase its own shares. It does not itself represent a contract to purchase those shares. A contingent purchase contract might arise, for example, where a shareholder is prepared to maintain an investment in a company only if there are arrangements that ensure that he will be able to sell his shares back to the company at any time in the future. In these circumstances, the company may not wish to issue a new class of redeemable shares in order to satisfy the shareholder's wishes. Instead, it may prefer to make a contractual arrangement with the shareholder under which the company may purchase the shares at a later date at the shareholder's option. Similarly, a contingent purchase contract would include, for example, a contract under which a company may be obliged to purchase an employee's shares on his retirement.

4.02 Such arrangements are not in themselves objectionable, but they are open to abuse unless they are accompanied by certain safeguards for other shareholders. The approach of the Companies Act 1981 is to treat contingent purchase contracts as if they were off-market contracts of purchase. This means that contingent purchase contracts require the same full range of safeguards for shareholders as apply to off-market contracts. A company may enter into a contingent purchase contract, or vary an existing contract, only after the terms of the contract, or any variation to the contract, have been approved by a special resolution of the company. Such approval may be varied, or revoked or renewed by a subsequent special resolution. The provisions discussed in paragraphs 2.18 to 2.20 and 3.08 and 3.09 in respect of a contract for an off-market purchase by a private company and a public company respectively apply also to contingent purchase contracts.

4.03   Paragraphs 2.22 and 3.17 discuss the requirements relating to the retention and the inspection of contingent purchase contracts, and any variation to the terms of any such contracts, that apply to private companies and public companies respectively.

The assignment or the release of a company's right to purchase its own shares

4.04   A company that has (with the requisite approval or authority) entered into a contract to make either a market purchase or an off-market purchase, or, alternatively, has entered into a contingent purchase contract, may not assign any rights that it acquires under the contract. This prohibition is designed to prevent a company from speculating against its own share price by buying and selling rights to purchase. The prohibition applies whether or not the shares are traded on the listed market or the Unlisted Securities Market of The Stock Exchange.

4.05   A company may release its rights under either a contract to make an off-market purchase or a contingent purchase contract only where the release has been approved in advance by a special resolution of the company. For this purpose, the requirements discussed in paragraphs 2.18 to 2.20 and 3.08 and 3.09 apply in respect of private companies and public companies respectively. Without such authorisation, any proposed release will be void.

4.06   In principle, there is nothing objectionable in allowing a company to release its rights of purchase. Circumstances may have changed since the time the contract was entered into. As a result, it may be advantageous to the company, and to the shareholder who has granted the right, and to the other members, for the purchase not to proceed. However, without certain safeguards, a company's release of its rights of purchase would provide it with an obvious means either to avoid the prohibition on assignment or to provide funds to a selected shareholder or group of shareholders at the expense of the others by buying a right to purchase their shares and then releasing the right. The main safeguard is the requirement for a special resolution.

Payments for transactions other than purchases

4.07   The Companies Act 1981 specifies certain circumstances in which any payment that a company makes must be out of its distributable profits. These circumstances are where the payment in question constitutes consideration for:

(a)   The acquisition of rights relating to a company's purchase of its own shares under a contingent purchase contract.

If the company pays the consideration for these rights otherwise than out of distributable profits, any subsequent purchase the company makes of its own shares under the contract will be unlawful.

(b)   The variation of either a contract to make an off-market purchase or a contingent purchase contract.

If the company pays the consideration for this variation otherwise than out of distributable profits, no subsequent purchase under the contract will be lawful.

(c)   The release of any of a company's obligations relating to its purchase of its own shares either under a contract to make a market purchase or an off-market purchase or under a contingent purchase contract.

If the company pays the consideration for the release otherwise than out of distributable profits, the purported release is void.

4.08   The object of this provision is to ensure that a company does not reduce its capital reserves in order to make a payment for an acquisition of rights, or a variation or a release.

The requirements of the City Code on Take-overs and Mergers

4.09   Whenever any public company wishes to purchase its own shares under the Companies Act 1981, it should discuss the matter in advance with the City Code Panel. This is because the Panel and the Council for the Securities Industry regard the Code as applying to the directors of all public companies resident in the UK, including the directors of those companies that are not listed.

The requirements of The Stock Exchange

4.10   The Quotations Department of The Stock Exchange has issued notes on the procedure that a listed company should follow when it proposes to purchase its own shares under the Companies Act 1981. The procedures are outlined in paragraphs 4.11 to 4.17.

4.11   The company must notify The Stock Exchange immediately the board decides to submit to the company's shareholders a proposal that the company should be authorised to purchase its own shares. The notification should indicate whether the proposal relates either to specific purchases or to a general authorisation to make purchases.

4.12   Where the company would purchase 15 per cent or more of its share capital if it exercised fully the authority it seeks, the company should treat the circular that seeks the shareholders' authority as a Class 1 circular for Stock Exchange purposes. Where this applies, the circular should comply with Schedule II, Part B of Admission of Securities to Listing (the "Yellow Book"). The working capital statement required should be based on the assumption that the company would use in full the authority it seeks at the maximum price specified (as discussed in paragraph 3.11). This assumption should be stated in the circular. In addition, where the authority the company seeks relates to specific proposals, the names of the shareholders who will be parties to the proposed contract should be stated. Also, all other material terms of the proposal should be stated. Where the board is seeking a general authority to purchase shares in the market, they should state their intentions with regard to the authority. They should notify shareholders if the company intends to 'stand in the market' either for a given period or until such time as it has acquired a specified number of shares.

The treatment of a company's purchase on the market by way of a 'put through' from a person with whom the company has a Class 4 relationship (for example, a director or a substantial shareholder) should be in accordance with the customary procedure for such transactions. (The procedure is given in Paragraph 8 of Chapter 4 of the Yellow Book.) This means that the company has to seek the shareholders' specific approval. A purchase from such a person outside The Stock Exchange would be an off-market purchase. Because it is such a purchase, the 1981 Act requires the shareholders to approve the terms of the purchase.

The company should immediately notify The Stock Exchange of the outcome of shareholders' meetings. It should forward to The Stock Exchange four copies of the relevant resolutions as soon as possible after the notification.

4.13 Where convertible securities or warrants or options to subscribe equity capital are in issue, the company should hold a separate class meeting of the holders to obtain their approval by extraordinary resolution before it either enters into any contract to purchase its own shares or first exercises a general authority to make purchases in the market. The company requires such approval whether or not there are provisions in the relevant trust deed or terms of issue in respect of adjustments to be made if the company were to purchase its own shares.

The circular containing the notice of meeting must set out clearly the apparent effect in terms of attributable assets and earnings on the expectations of the holders on conversion or subscription if the company were to exercise fully the authorisation that it seeks to purchase its own shares. In addition, any special adjustments that the company may propose should be set out. All the above information should be restated on the revised basis.

4.14 Where, within a period of 12 months, the company purchases 5 per cent or more of its share capital, it should make these purchases by way of either a tender offer or a partial offer to all shareholders.

The company should make the tender offer on The Stock Exchange at a stated maximum price. In addition, the company should give notice of the offer by means of a paid advertisement in two national newspapers at least seven days before the offer closes. A company is advised to consult its stockbroker for advice on the procedures for such offers.

4.15 The model code for directors should be regarded as applying to a company's purchases of its own shares. Consequently, a company should not purchase its own shares at any time when its directors would not be free to do so on their own account.

4.16 The company should notify to The Stock Exchange all its purchases of its own shares by midday on the dealing day following the day of the purchase. The notification should include the number of shares purchased, and either the purchase price per share or the highest and lowest prices paid. Details of these notifications will appear in The Stock Exchange Weekly Official Intelligence.

4.17   In addition to giving the details in respect of purchases that the Companies Act 1981 requires to be disclosed in the directors' report (as discussed in paragraph 2.23), a company should give similar information in respect of any purchases it has made of its own shares since the end of the year covered by the report. The directors' report should also contain particulars of any authorities or approvals the shareholders gave to the board that exist at the end of the financial year. The particulars in the directors' report should include the names of the sellers for all purchases the company has made, or has proposed to make, otherwise than through the market, or has made by tender or by partial offer to all shareholders.

Part V

This part contains comments on acquisitions other than purchases and, in particular, on redeemable shares.

Acquisitions other than purchases

5.01 A company can not only purchase its own shares. It can also acquire them by:

(a) Redemption (that is, where shares are given a fixed life on issue and are redeemed at the end of that life).

(b) Repayment (that is, where the company and the shareholders agree, and the court consents, that the shares should be repaid).

Although the three different methods by which a company can acquire its own shares are technically different in company law, they are all treated in the same way for tax purposes. Whether the company acquires the shares by purchase, or by redemption, or by repayment, the favourable tax treatment is available — provided that the company meets the qualifying conditions.

5.02 The Companies Act 1981 did not alter the provisions on repayment, but it did alter the provisions in respect of redeemable shares. Accordingly, the issue and the redemption of redeemable shares are considered in the following paragraphs.

Redeemable shares

5.03 Section 58 of the Companies Act 1948 enabled companies to issue redeemable *preference* shares. The Companies Act 1981 replaces section 58 with provisions that (subject to certain restrictions) enable all companies with a share capital to issue redeemable shares of any class. There are certain provisions that relate to redeemable shares issued before 15 June 1982 and these are covered in paragraph 5.16.

The issue of redeemable shares.

5.04 Any company that has a share capital may, if it is authorised to do so by its articles of association, issue redeemable shares subject to the restriction discussed in paragraph 5.05. Redeemable shares include shares that are to be redeemed on a particular date, as well as shares that are merely liable to be redeemed at the option of either the company or a shareholder.

5.05   There is, however, an important restriction on this power. A company may issue redeemable shares only if it has in issue shares that are not redeemable. (Paragraph 2.04 gives an explanation of this condition.)

The redemption of redeemable shares.

5.06   A company may not redeem shares unless those shares are fully paid.

5.07   The terms of the redemption must provide for the company to make payment at the time that the shares are redeemed. (Paragraph 2.07 gives an explanation of this condition.)

5.08   All companies may, in general, redeem redeemable shares either out of distributable profits or out of the proceeds of a new issue of shares the company has made for the purposes of the redemption. A private company may, in addition, make a payment out of capital to redeem shares, provided that it is authorised to do so by its articles of association. The provisions in respect of a company's purchase of its own shares out of capital discussed in paragraphs 2.24 to 2.48 apply equally to a redemption of shares out of capital.

5.09   The treatment of a premium payable on redemption is the same as that of a premium payable on purchase as discussed in paragraph 2.09.

5.10   The terms of the redemption may be set out in the company's articles of association, but the articles must not conflict in any way with the provisions of the Companies Act 1981. This provision is in contrast to the situation where a company purchases its own shares. The reason for the difference is that, with a purchase, it will not normally be possible to foresee at the time when a company's articles of association are being formulated the circumstances under which that company may wish to purchase its shares. On the other hand, the very nature of redeemable shares means that this uncertainty should not apply.

5.11   A company must treat shares as being cancelled on redemption. Thus, the redemption of shares will reduce the issued share capital by the nominal amount of the shares redeemed. However, the redemption will not reduce the authorised share capital.

5.12   The provisions in respect of the maintenance of capital discussed in paragraphs 2.49 to 2.58 apply equally to a redemption of shares.

The issue of shares for the purposes of a redemption.

5.13   The provisions are the same as those for the issue of shares for the purposes of a purchase as discussed in paragraphs 2.14 to 2.16.

A company's failure to redeem shares.

5.14   The provisions are the same as those in respect of a company's failure to purchase shares as discussed in paragraph 2.59.

The effect of a winding up on a company's obligation to redeem shares.

5.15 The provisions are the same as those in respect of the effect of a winding up on the obligation to purchase shares as discussed in paragraph 2.60.

Transitional provisions.

5.16 Where a company issued redeemable preference shares before 15 June 1982, those shares will be redeemable in accordance with the provisions of the Companies Act 1981. However, any premium that is payable on the redemption of those shares may be paid wholly or partly out of the share premium account, and the provisions discussed in paragraph 2.09 do not apply.

Part VI

This part contains a discussion of several important practical points that may emerge from the implementation of the tax law provisions.

Introduction

6.01 The tax legislation about companies purchasing their own shares is new. Experience of its implementation and effects in practice is necessarily limited. However, several important practical points have already emerged, and it is these points that are discussed in this part of the booklet.

The practical points fall conveniently into two categories: those that affect the company's tax position and those that affect the shareholder's tax position.

The company's tax position

6.02 The points that have emerged in respect of a company that purchases its own shares are concerned mainly with tax relief for the various expenses incurred by the company.

Tax relief for the purchase price.

6.03 Before the new legislation was enacted the amount by which the purchase price exceeded the nominal value of the shares would have been treated as a dividend. Such a payment is regarded as an appropriation of profits, and it is not tax deductible. The same rule applies if the purchase price is treated as a dividend under the new legislation.

6.04 The new legislation permits the share purchase to be a disposal for capital gains purposes provided that the qualifying conditions are satisfied. So far as the company is concerned, the payment would be on capital account, and it would not be deductible for its own tax purposes.

Tax relief for interest.

6.05 A company that purchases its own shares may not have liquid funds available to pay the purchase price, and so it may borrow the necessary funds. The typical case will involve a trading company borrowing from its bankers in the UK. To obtain tax relief for the interest on the borrowed funds the company would have to show that the payment of interest was made wholly and exclusively for the purposes of the trade. In the way in which this test has been interpreted in various cases before the courts it is not clear that it is similar to the requirement under the new rules that the sole or main purpose of the transaction should be to benefit the company's trade. Accordingly, although the terms of the two tests are similar, we consider that tax relief is not necessarily available.

Tax relief for costs.

6.06   A company's purchase of its own shares will inevitably involve professional costs for matters such as clearance applications and legal documentation. For the reasons stated above in paragraph 6.05 we consider that these costs might not be tax deductible for the company. The reason for this view is that the costs are incurred in connection with the company's purchase of its own shares. To meet the requirements of the new legislation the sole or main purpose of the purchase must be to benefit the company's trade. Accordingly, the costs might not satisfy the requirement for a tax deduction (namely, that they were expended *wholly and exclusively* for the purposes of the company's trade).

6.07   It is interesting to note that if the company's payment for its own shares is treated as a dividend, there is less scope for arguing that costs should be tax deductible. As mentioned in paragraph 6.03, a dividend is an appropriation of profits. Costs incurred in connection with appropriating profits cannot be said to be incurred in earning those profits. It is unlikely, therefore, that such costs would satisfy the requirement of being incurred wholly and exclusively for the purposes of the company's trade. Consequently, they would not be tax deductible. However, even if the company's payment is treated as a dividend, the interest on any bank borrowings to fund the payment would be deductible as a charge on income.

Shortfall apportionments.

6.08   Where a company is owned by a few shareholders it may be liable to have its non-trading income apportioned to its shareholders. That is, both the company and its shareholders are taxed as if the company had paid a dividend equal in amount to its non-trading income. Such a company is known as a "close company". The company can resist this tax treatment if it can show that it needs to retain the funds for business purposes.

6.09   It is not clear whether a company could resist a shortfall apportionment on the grounds that it wanted to build up a cash fund in order to purchase its own shares in the future. Unfortunately, it is impossible to give a general view on this matter because each case will depend upon its own facts. However, a mere vague intention on the part of the company to purchase its own shares at some time in the future would probably not be sufficient. There should at least be a definite proposal for the company to acquire the shares, although even such a proposal may not be sufficient in certain circumstances. In particular, if the shares the company is purchasing are those it issued at the start of business, the company could not avoid a shortfall apportionment.

Stamp duty.

6.10   A straightforward sale of shares involves a liability to stamp duty of 2 per cent of the purchase price. When a company cancels shares, however, it incurs no liability to stamp duty.

Where a company purchases its own shares there is first a purchase and then an immediate cancellation of the shares. There appears to be scope for argument about the possible stamp duty involved. However, during the debates on the Companies Acts in Parliament, an amendment was introduced that was designed to prevent a liability to stamp duty arising.

The shareholder's tax position

6.11   The practical points that have emerged in connection with the shareholder's tax position are concerned with the possible impact other legislation has on the sale of the shares to the company.

Anti-avoidance legislation.

6.12   Legislation was introduced in 1960 to prevent shareholders extracting accumulated funds from companies in a form that did not bear income tax. That legislation is now found in the Income and Corporation Taxes Act 1970, section 460. In certain circumstances, that legislation could apply to a transaction whereby a company purchases its own shares. However, a clearance procedure is available under section 460, and we consider that if the company satisfies the requirements in the Finance Act 1982, then it should obtain a clearance under section 460. Appendix VI shows that a single clearance application can be made in respect of the new rules under the Finance Act 1982 and the Income and Corporation Taxes Act 1970, section 460.

6.13   Neither the Companies Act 1981 nor the Finance Act 1982 makes any reference to a valuation of the shares the company purchases. In practice, the value will normally be a figure agreed among the shareholders. Care should always be taken in setting the value of the shares because the Capital Gains Tax Act 1979 contains provisions to counter tax avoidance by fixing artificial valuations for shares. Unfortunately, there is no clearance procedure under these provisions, and the Inland Revenue have declined to confirm that the provisions would never be applied. However, we consider that if the amount the company pays is a reasonable and fair price, then these anti-avoidance provisions should not apply.

Treatment of the price as a dividend or a capital gain.

6.14   If the company satisfies the qualifying conditions, the price a shareholder receives (less his acquisition cost) is taxed as a capital gain. However, it may not always be to the taxpayer's advantage for capital gains tax to be charged. In some cases it will be obvious which treatment is preferable. If the dividend would be taxed at the top rate of income tax of 75 per cent and the capital gain at only 30 per cent then the shareholder would clearly prefer capital gains treatment.

6.15   Sometimes, however, the choice is not so clear cut. The shareholder may have tax reliefs or allowances to set against the dividend, or he may be taxed at a lower rate than the top rate of 75 per cent. Conversely, if the amount involved is modest then the annual exemption from capital gains tax of £5,000 may be a significant factor. These various factors make it difficult to give general rules. However, the following guidelines may prove useful in practice:

(a)   If the dividend would be taxed at a rate lower than 30 per cent it is preferable for the company's payment to be taxed as a dividend.

(b)   If the dividend would be taxed at a rate higher than 51 per cent it is preferable for the company's payment to be taxed as a capital gain.

(c)   If the dividend would be taxed at rates between 30 per cent and 51 per cent it would be necessary to make a precise calculation of the income tax and capital gains tax liabilities to determine the more advantageous treatment.

6.16   One further factor needs to be borne in mind in this connection. Once a capital gain is realised it is extremely difficult to shelter it from tax. Conversely, there are various forms of tax shelter available that could be used to mitigate the potential tax liability on the company's payment if it were treated as a dividend. It is not possible to explore this matter in detail here because expert professional advice will be required in each case.

Tax relief provided by the business start-up scheme.

6.17   In 1981, a radical new tax relief was introduced. Provided that various conditions are satisfied, a taxpayer who subscribes for shares in a new trading company can deduct the amount invested (within prescribed limits) from his income for tax purposes. The new relief is called the "business start-up scheme".

6.18   The new legislation that allows companies to purchase their own shares should overcome one of the major practical disadvantages of the business start-up scheme. One of the qualifying conditions of the scheme is that the investor should have only a minority interest. It has proved difficult in practice to find buyers for such shareholdings. Under the new legislation the company itself can purchase the shares.

APPENDIX I

Checklist of the requirements of the Companies Act 1981 that apply when either a private company or a public company purchases its own shares

This checklist is designed to assist a company to ensure that it has satisfied all of the relevant conditions of, and the detailed procedures specified by, the Companies Act 1981 when it purchases its own shares. The conditions and procedures for a private company and for a public company are explained in Part II and Part III respectively of the booklet.

The reference against each step in the checklist is a reference to the relevant section of the Companies Act 1981.

	Reference	Yes/ No/ N/A
Conditions to be satisfied		
1. Do the company's articles of association authorise it to purchase its own shares?	Sec 46(1)	....
2. After the purchase, will the company have at least some shares in issue that are not redeemable?	Sec 46(3)	....
3. After the purchase will the company have at least two members (as required by the Companies Acts 1948 and 1980)?		....
4. After the purchase will a *public* company's allotted share capital exceed the authorised minimum required by the Companies Act 1980?		....
5. Are the shares to be purchased fully paid?	Secs 45(3), 46(2)	....
6. Do the terms of purchase provide for payment to be made at the time that the shares are purchased?	Secs 45(4), 46(2)	....
7. Is the payment by a *private* company either out of distributable profits, or out of the proceeds of a new issue of shares the company has made for the purposes of the purchase, or out of capital?	Secs 45(5)(a), 46(2), 54	....
Note: Appendix III gives the conditions a company needs to satisfy where it makes a payment out of capital.		
8. Is the payment by a *public* company either out of distributable profits or out of the proceeds of a new issue of shares the company has made for the purposes of the purchase?	Secs 45(5)(a), 46(2)	....

53

	Reference	Yes/ No/ N/A
9. Is the premium, if any, payable on the purchase correctly treated (see paragraph 2.09)?	Secs 45(5)(b), (6), 46(2)	....
10. Will the shares be cancelled on purchase?	Secs 45(8), 46(2)	....

Procedures for off-market purchases

11. Have the terms of the proposed contract been authorised by a special resolution of the company (see paragraphs 2.18 and 2.19)?	Sec 47(5)	....
12. Has any proposed variation to an existing contract been authorised by a special resolution?	Sec 47(11)	....
13. Does the authority given by a special resolution of a *public* company specify a date on which the authority expires, and is this date no later than 18 months from the date of the resolution?	Sec 47(7), (8)	....
14. For the special resolution to be effective, have certain documents been made available for inspection (see paragraph 2.20)?	Sec 47(10), (11)	....

Procedures for market purchases (public companies only)

15. Has the proposed purchase been authorised by an ordinary resolution of the company in general meeting?	Sec 49(3)	....
16. Does the authority:		
(a) Specify the maximum number of shares that may be acquired?	Sec 49(5)(a)	....
(b) Determine both the maximum and the minimum prices that the company may pay for the shares (see paragraph 3.11)?	Sec 49(5)(b), (9)	....
(c) Specify the date on which it expires? Also, is this date within 18 months of the date of the resolution (see paragraph 3.11)?	Sec 49(5)(c), (7)	....
17. Has any variation to the authority been authorised by an ordinary resolution?	Sec 49(6)	....
18. Has a copy of any resolution been sent to the Registrar of Companies within 15 days of it being passed?	Sec 49(10)	....

	Reference	Yes/ No/ N/A

Disclosure of a company's purchase of its own shares

19.   Within 28 days of the date that shares purchased are delivered to the company, has the company made a return in the prescribed form to the Registrar of Companies (see paragraphs 2.21 and 3.16)?   Sec 52(1)   ....

20.   Will the company keep certain documents at its registered office for 10 years (see paragraph 2.22)?   Sec 52(4), (9)   ....

21.   Will the directors' report in respect of the year in which the purchases took place include details of the purchases (see paragraph 2.23)?   Sec 14   ....

Note: Paragraph 4.17 gives the additional details that a listed company needs to disclose in its directors' report to satisfy the requirements of The Stock Exchange.

Maintenance of capital

22.   Has the company made the appropriate transfer to the capital redemption reserve (see paragraphs 2.50 to 2.53)?   Sec 53   ....

APPENDIX II

Prescribed form for a return by a company purchasing its own shares

Form No. 64

THE COMPANIES ACTS 1948 TO 1981

Return by a company purchasing its own shares

Pursuant to section 52(1)(2) and (3) of the Companies Act 1981

Please do not write in this binding margin

Please complete legibly, preferably in black type, or bold block lettering

Note
This return must be delivered to the registrar within a period of 28 days beginning with the first date on which shares to which it relates were delivered to the company.

* Insert full name of company

To the Registrar of Companies

For official use

Company Number

Name of company

*

The return of shares purchased by the company under section 46 of the Companies Act 1981 is as follows : —

Class of shares				
Number of shares purchased				
Nominal value of the shares				
Date(s) on which the shares were delivered to the company				
Maximum and minimum prices paid for the shares †	max min			

† A private company is not required to give this information

The aggregate amount paid by the company for the shares to which this return relates was: _____ †

‡ Delete as appropriate

Signed   [Director] [Secretary] ‡   Date

Presentor's name, address and reference (if any): —

For official use
General section   Post room

56

Checklist of the requirements of the Companies Act 1981 that apply when a private company purchases its own shares out of capital

This checklist is designed to assist a private company to ensure that it has satisfied all of the relevant conditions of the Companies Act 1981 when it purchases its own shares out of capital. The conditions are explained in Part II of the booklet.

The reference against each step in the checklist is a reference to the relevant section of the Companies Act 1981.

	Reference	Yes/ No/ N/A
1. Do the company's articles of association authorise it to make a payment out of capital?	Sec 54(1)	....
2. Does the payment not exceed the permissible capital payment (see paragraphs 2.34 to 2.37)?	Sec 54(2), (3)	....
3. Have the directors of the company made a statutory declaration in the prescribed form (see paragraph 2.28)?	Sec 55(3), (4), (5)	....
4. Have the auditors made a report addressed to the directors (see paragraph 2.29)?	Sec 55(5)	....
5. Has the payment been approved by a special resolution passed on, or within one week after, the date on which the directors made the statutory declaration (see paragraphs 2.30 and 2.31)?	Sec 55(2), (6), (7), (8)	....
6. Is the payment to be made not earlier than five weeks, nor later than seven weeks, after the date of the resolution?	Sec 55(6)	....
7. Has the company given the required publicity in respect of the payment (see paragraphs 2.38 to 2.41)?	Sec 56	....

APPENDIX IV

Prescribed form for a declaration in relation to the redemption or purchase of shares out of capital

G

THE COMPANIES ACTS 1948 TO 1981

Declaration in relation to the redemption or purchase of shares out of capital

Pursuant to section 55(3)(4) and (5)
of the Companies Act 1981.

Please do not write in this binding margin

Please complete legibly, preferably in black type or bold block lettering.

Note:
Please read the notes on page 4 before completing this form.

* Delete as appropriate
† See note 1 delete either or both if inappropriate

‡ See note 2

For official use   Company number

Name of company

Limited

[being a   [recognised bank]   *

[licensed institution]   *   within the meaning of the Banking Act 1979] †

[being authorised to carry on insurance business in the United Kingdom] †

proposes to make a payment in respect of the [redemption] [purchase] * of its own shares out of capital, that is, otherwise than out of distributable profits ‡ of the company or the proceeds of a fresh issue of shares.

Overleaf

Presentor's name, address and reference (if any):

For official use
General section   Post room

58

Therefore [I] [we] *
(NOTE 3)

Please do not
write in this
binding margin

⟱

Please complete
legibly, preferably
in black type or
bold block lettering.

* Delete as
appropriate

Name Address
Name Address
Name Address
Name Address
Name Address
Name Address
Name Address
Name Address
Name Address
Name Address

being all the directors of the company do solemnly and sincerely declare that: —

(1) the amount of the permissible capital payment* proposed to be made for the shares in question is £

(2) having made full inquiry into the affairs and prospects of the company [I] [we] † have formed the opinion :-

(a) as regards its initial situation immediately following the date on which the payment out of capital is proposed to be made, that there will be no ground on which the company could then be found to be unable to pay its debts ‡ and

(b) as regards its prospects for the year immediately following that date, that, having regard to [my] [our] † intentions with respect to the management of the company's business during that year and to the amount and character of the financial resources which will in [my] [our] † view be available to the company during that year, the company will be able to continue to carry on business as a going concern (and will accordingly be able to pay its debts as they fall due) throughout that year.

And [I] [we] † make this solemn declaration conscientiously believing the same to be true and by virtue of the provisions of the Statutory Declarations Act 1835.

Signature(s) of Declarant(s)

Declared at ————————————— ⎞
————————————————— |
————————————————— |
the ———day of ——————— ⎬
one thousand nine hundred and ——— |
————————————————— |
before me ————————————— ⎠
A Commissioner for Oaths, or Notary
Public or Justice of the Peace or Solicitor
having the powers conferred on a
Commissioner for Oaths.

Notes

1   This is the information with respect to the nature of the business of the company prescribed pursuant to section 55(5) of the Companies Act 1981.
Delete either or both if inappropriate.

2   The term 'distributable profits' is defined in section 62(1) of the Companies Act 1981.

3   Insert the full names and addresses of all the directors of the company.

4   'Permissible capital payment' means the amount which, taken together with
    (i) any available profits of the company; and
    (ii) the proceeds of any fresh issue of shares made for the purposes of the redemption or purchase;
is equal to the price of redemption or purchase.
'Available profits' means the company's profits which are available for distribution (within the meaning of Part III of the Companies Act 1980);
the question whether a company has any profits so available and the amount of any such profits is to be determined in accordance with section 54(8)–(10) of the Companies Act 1981.

5   Contingent and prospective liabilities of the company must be taken into account, see section 223(d) of the Companies Act 1948 and section 55(4) of the Companies Act 1981.

6   A copy of this declaration must be delivered to the registrar together with a copy of the auditors report required by section 55(5) of the Companies Act 1981: see section 56(4) of the Companies Act 1981.

APPENDIX V

Prescribed form for a notice of application to the court for the cancellation of a resolution for the redemption of purchase of shares out of capital

THE COMPANIES ACTS 1948 TO 1981

Form No. 66

Notice of application to the court for the cancellation of a resolution for the redemption or purchase of shares out of capital

Please do not write in this binding margin

Please complete legibly, preferably in black type, or bold block lettering.

Pursuant to section 57(3)(a) of the Companies Act 1981

To the Registrar of Companies

For official use

Company number

Name of Company

Limited

hereby gives you notice in accordance with section 57(3)(a) of the Companies Act 1981 that an application has been made to the court under section 57(1) of that Act for the cancellation of the special resolution for payment out of capital for the redemption or purchase of some of the company's shares dated _____

a copy of which was sent to you on _____

† Delete as appropriate

Signed   [Director] [Secretary] †   Date

Presentor's name, address and reference (if any):

For official use
General section   Post room

62

Application for clearance under Finance Act 1982, Schedule 9, Paragraphs 10(1) and 10(2)

Procedure

Applications should be sent to:

> Inland Revenue
> Technical Division (Company Taxation)
> Room 28
> New Wing
> Somerset House
> London WC2R 1LB

Where appropriate clearance may also be sought under section 464, Income and Corporation Taxes Act 1970. Applications under section 464 should be sent to:

> Inland Revenue
> Technical Division
> Room 411
> Melbourne House
> Aldwych
> London WC2B 4LL

If preferred, a single application may be made under both provisions. The application should then be directed to Room 28, New Wing, Somerset House, with an extra copy of the application and enclosures for each additional clearance sought.

Form of application

To assist companies in preparing clearance applications under Paragraphs 10(1) and 10(2) and to facilitate their consideration by the Board an outline of the basic information needed is given below. It is not an exhaustive statement and each applicant in giving the particulars of the relevant transactions required by Paragraph 10(3) must fully and accurately disclose all facts and circumstances material for the decision of the Board (Paragraph 10(6)). In what follows, references to purchase of shares include references to repayment or redemption.

Application for clearance under Paragraph 10(1)

Section 53(1) and Schedule 9 contain conditions which must be satisfied, where applicable, before the new tax treatment afforded by section 53(1) can apply. A comprehensive application which has regard to each of these conditions will remove the need for lengthy fact-finding enquiries and enable the Board to come to a decision on the application with the minimum of delay.

The advice below refers only to applications under Paragraph 10(1). Where a single application is made under that and other provisions it should open by stating clearly the provisions under which it is made and should be expanded to include any additional information needed for the application(s) under the other provision(s).

It will be helpful if applications follow the order set out below, each item being expanded as necessary and any further information being added at the end.

A.   **Section 53(1) or (2), Finance Act 1982.**

It should be stated at the outset whether the purchase of own shares is regarded as falling within Finance Act 1982, section 53(1) or section 53(2). If the purchasing company or any company which is, or was at the time, a member of the same 51 per cent group as the purchasing company has previously made an application under Paragraph 10(1) the Board's reference(s) should be quoted.

B.   **Purchases within Section 53(1).**

1.   **Company.**

(a)   The name of the company making the purchase.

(b)   Its Tax District and reference.

(c)   Confirmation that it is an unquoted company as defined (Paragraph 16(1), Schedule 9).

(d)   Its status, ie "trading company" or "the holding company of a trading group" within the Paragraph 16(1), Schedule 9 definitions or some other type of company not within the definitions.

2.   **Groups.**

Where the company is a member of a group (see below):

(a)   The names of the group companies together with their Tax Districts and references.

(b)   A statement or diagram showing the shareholding interests of each group company in other group companies.

A group for the purpose of this paragraph is the largest 51 per cent group to which the purchasing company belongs (Paragraph 5(7), Schedule 9), but the meaning of "group" is extended, where appropriate by Paragraph 5(8) and (10), Schedule 9.

3.   **Shareholders.**

(a)   A list of the current shareholders in the purchasing company, and where appropriate, in each company in a group as in 2. above, together with particulars (amount, class, dividend rights, etc.) of their current holdings.

(b)   A statement of any relationships of the shareholders to each other.

(c)   Where a shareholder is the son or daughter of another shareholder, an indication that he or she is over 18. If he or she is under 18, please give details of their age.

4.   **Prior transactions.**

Particulars of any prior transactions or re-arrangements in preparation for the purchase.

5.   **Proposed purchase.**

Details of the shares to be purchased, the purchase price and the method of payment.

6.   **Purpose and benefits.**

A statement of the reasons for the purchase, the trading benefits expected and any other benefits expected to accrue whether or not to the purchasing company.

7.   **Section 53(1) (b) conditions.**

Confirmation together with all relevant information that the purchase etc. does not form part of a scheme or arrangement the main purpose or one of the main purposes of which is to enable the owner of the shares to participate in the profits of the company without receiving a dividend, or the avoidance of tax.

8.   Certain conditions are set out in Schedule 9. In order to show that these conditions will be satisfied, where appropriate, you should indicate with supporting calculations where necessary:

(a)   (i)   The present residence status of the vendor and any intended changes (Paragraph 1).

(ii)   The Tax District and reference of each vendor, and if not known the address of the vendor's private residence in the UK. (Paragraph 1).

(b)   The period of ownership by the vendor of the shares to be purchased (Paragraph 3).

(c)   If appropriate, that the vendor's interest will be "substantially reduced" (Paragraph 3).

(d)   If appropriate, that the combined interests as shareholders of the vendor and his associates will be substantially reduced (Paragraph 4).

(e)   If appropriate, that the vendor's interest as a shareholder in the group will be substantially reduced (Paragraph 5).

(f)   If appropriate, that the combined interests as shareholders in the group of the vendor and his associates will be substantially reduced (Paragraph 6).

(g)   That the vendor will immediately after the purchase, not be connected with the company making the purchase or with any company which is a member of the same group as that company (Paragraphs 7 and 15).

(h)   That the purchase is not part of a scheme or arrangement within Paragraph 8 of Schedule 9.

9.   **Balance sheet and profit and loss account.**

The latest available balance sheet and profit and loss account for the purchasing company and for any group (see paragraph 2. above) companies and in the case of a 51 per cent group the consolidated balance sheet and profit and loss account, together with a note of any material relevant changes between the balance sheet date and the proposed purchase etc.

C.   **Purchase within Section 53(2).**

1.   **Company.**

(a)   The name of the company making the purchase.

(b)   Its Tax District and reference.

(c)   Confirmation that it is unquoted (Paragraph 16(1), Schedule 9).

(d)   Its status, i.e. "trading company" or "the holding company of a trading group" within the Paragraph 16(1), Schedule 9, definitions or some other type of company not within the definitions.

2.   **Groups.**

Where appropriate.

(a)   The names of the group companies together with their Tax Districts and references.

(b)   A statement or diagram showing the shareholding interest of each group company in other group companies.

A group for this purpose is the largest 75 per cent group to which the purchasing company belongs.

3.   **Proposed purchase.**

Details of the shares to be purchased, the purchase price and method of payment.

4.   **Capital transfer tax.**

(a)   The name and date of death of the deceased.

(b)   The reference of the deceased at the Capital Tax Office.

(c)   The amount of the outstanding tax and whether or not liability has been finally agreed.

(d)   The extent to which the purchase price is to be applied in satisfaction of the tax liability.

(e)   A full explanation of the circumstances in which there would be "undue hardship" if the tax liability were to be discharged otherwise than through the purchase of own shares from this or another such company.

5.   **Balance sheet and profit and loss account.**

The latest available balance sheet and profit and loss account for the purchasing company and for any group companies and in the case of a group the consolidated balance sheet and profit and loss account, together with a note of any material relevant changes between the balance sheet date and the proposed purchase etc.

Application for clearance under Paragraph 10(2)

1.   **Company.**

(a)   The name of the company making the purchase.

(b)   Its Tax District and reference.

(c)   The latest available balance sheet and profit and loss account for the company and for any group companies and in the case of a group the consolidated balance sheet and profit and loss account, together with a note of any material relevant changes between the balance sheet date and the proposed purchase.

2. **Proposed purchase.**

Details of the shares to be purchased, the purchase price and the method of payment.

3. A statement of the reasons why it is believed the proposed payment does not fall within the provisions of Section 53, Finance Act 1982.